SMOOTH SAILING ON ROUGH SEAS

8 Principles of High-Performance Business

Strategies for hardwiring your people and management practices into your company's business performance

Rob Rose

With **Shannon Ross**

Introduction by **Ron Zambonini**
President and CEO, Cognos Incorporated

Foreword by **Dr. Fariborz Ghadar**
Director, Center for Global Business Studies,
Pennsylvania State University

Published by Cognos Press, 3755 Riverside Drive, P.O. Box 9707, Station T, Ottawa, ON, Canada K1G 4K9.
Cognos and the Cognos logo are trademarks or registered trademarks of Cognos Incorporated in the United States and/or other countries.
All others are the property of their respective trademark holders.

Printed in Canada, 2002.

ISBN 0-9730124-0-4

CONTENTS

Foreword v

Introduction 1

Moving from Process Efficiency to Performance Management 3

The Smart and the Fast 9

Principles of High-Performance Business 17

    High-Performance People 21

    High-Performance Practices 41

    High-Performance Management 59

Conclusion 78

Case Study: Imagine…Going from Discovery to Action in Five Days 81

Acknowledgments 103

In the 21st-century economy, achieving sustainable business success is already proving to be a greater challenge than ever before, regardless of the industry in which an organization operates. Shaping a coherent strategy for consistently high business performance has never been so crucial, or so complex.

From a business perspective, the legacy of the 20th century is one of rapidly changing markets and dramatically accelerated product life cycles. The latter have shrunk from the luxurious 15- to 20-year cycles of 50 years ago to a mere two to three years today. In addition, product development costs have skyrocketed more than tenfold during the same time period. And it has become increasingly more difficult to generate the healthy return on R&D investment required to develop new products, processes, and services.

Companies went through the reengineering and downsizing in the 1980s to become leaner, meaner, and more efficient only to be faced with the globalization and accelerated pace of business heralded in the 1990s. "We realized that we needed to take our products global very quickly, gain market share, and hopefully make our product or service the standard of the industry in order to recoup the rising cost of product development in shorter and shorter life cycles." This is a statement heard from many a CEO in the past decade.

Companies today realize that to achieve the effectiveness they are seeking they also need the ability to respond quickly to often changing market needs. They need the ability to act quickly and intelligently—right across the organization.

Astute companies have realized that accomplishing this requires two interconnected actions. First, managers and decision-makers at all levels of the firm need to share accurate and thorough information about the business. Second, they need to develop a collective understanding of the critical factors of business success. They can then coordinate and align their decision-making—and do wonderfully effective things for their organization. It's not too much to say that the forward-looking, winning company has become a true "learning corporation," which not only shares and disseminates information throughout all levels within the firm but also effectively implements its distilled responses.

But ensuring that everyone within the organization can act quickly and intelligently is only the starting point to meeting the challenge of developing new products, producing and distributing them efficiently, and then successfully marketing them on a global scale. Companies in industries ranging from automotive to telecommunications to computing to pharmaceutical to financial services are increasingly forming alliances to acquire market presence and investment resources. And they are outsourcing business processes and activities that are core elements in their value proposition.

Global success today requires an integrated organization that moves into markets with speed and flexibility. If you can't do it alone, partner with others where you lack the superior core capability or best-in-class processes. Focus your operations on core competencies, and benchmark to be certain about your position. Today's business survival and competitiveness depend on the efficiency and effectiveness of the organization's entire value chain. Integration and collaboration have become key business imperatives. Business performance management must be distributed to the closest point of impact across the whole value chain.

This new business paradigm requires sharing of timely information and implementing responses not just within the firm itself but also among its key strategic alliances.

Organizations must ensure that "their" people—who now extend across a complex value chain of partners and suppliers—are given the proper information and analytic skills and tools and are encouraged and empowered to respond quickly to the customer. Organizations that are successful are the ones that are able to pull all of this off. This book outlines the key strategies necessary to do so.

In Smooth Sailing on Rough Seas, Rob Rose has identified the principles of high-performance business to guide managers to address the challenges they face in this era of distributed decision-making. Mr. Rose, a vice president of Cognos Incorporated, shares his many years of experience working with some of the world's high-performance enterprises: companies that have found ways to align their business planning and execution within and across functions throughout their firm and across their strategic alliances—companies that, as a result, have forged ahead of the competition.

This book is essential reading for executives and managers and excels in setting out the management imperative for performance-driven decision-making across value chains. It makes a compelling case for distributing business performance management to the closest point of impact and proposes eight tangible principles that are fundamental to performance-driven decision-making in today's rapidly changing business environment.

Dr. Fariborz Ghadar
William A. Schreyer Professor of Global Management, Policies and Planning
and Director, Center for Global Business Studies, Pennsylvania State University

High-performance companies get it.

They understand how and where people and performance intersect. They understand that good business performance reflects effective decisions—both tactical and strategic. And they understand that to make effective, confident decisions, people need consistent, accessible information they can rely on all the time.

For many years, we at Cognos have had the pleasure of working with some of the world's high-performance enterprises. These are the companies that have forged ahead of their competitors because they've found ways to tightly align their business planning with execution within and across functions. They have achieved major breakthroughs—in reducing costs and accelerating throughput but, more importantly, in customer satisfaction, innovation, and value creation.

High-performance companies recognize that there is more to performance than outrunning the competition. For them, winning starts with strategy and planning. They run smarter and play the game better than anyone else. And so, they have built their business models to be agile and flexible. They have created cultures that embrace change. And these companies have found ways to empower everyone—from the boardroom to the shop floor—to achieve peak performance in this age of unprecedented transformation. They use information to propel the business and empower the people who make performance happen.

Most organizations today have already implemented operational systems to automate and help better manage key functions and processes—human resources systems, general ledger systems, order entry systems, and so on. However, as critical as they are to running the business, these systems simply level the playing field.

I believe that the next level of competitive advantage—and the next breakthrough in productivity—will come from companies better connecting their people to the business, its vision, its strategy, and its performance, so that the organization as a whole can focus on achieving a single outcome: winning the race.

Over the years, we've observed many examples of leadership that encompass the defining characteristics of a high-performance company. From giving people access to the information they need to make effective decisions, to connecting them with other decision-makers who impact performance, both inside and outside of the organization. From ensuring all of these people are tapping into information that is consistent and relevant across the board, to facilitating their collaboration in ways that are designed to drive performance. From paying attention to non-financial drivers that are critical to solid execution, to creating a culture that pushes decision-making to the closest point of impact. These concepts can be applied in any company, large or small, to improve business performance in its organization.

It is a great pleasure to see key aspects of that experience distilled and shared in the pages that follow. The eight principles put forward in this book offer actionable, foundational strategies for hardwiring agility, flexibility, and innovation into a company—and becoming a high-performance business.

Ron Zambonini
President and CEO
Cognos Incorporated

Moving from
Process Efficiency
to Performance
Management

In the beginning, there was paper. And, until recently, it was paper that drove the processes that powered the business: purchase orders, product spec sheets, timesheets, memos, manuals, and a plethora of financial and accounting documentation. The list goes on and on.

Then, in the latter half of the 20th century, technology innovators like IBM brought to market transactional systems that made it possible for businesses to automate many of these paper-based activities. While most of these systems focused on operational processes—general ledger systems, manufacturing systems, and so on—companies discovered that by investing in automation technologies, they could noticeably increase their efficiency by reducing their dependency on time-consuming paper-based processes.

The goal of increasing efficiency was—and, in many cases, still is—addressing phenomena such as the so-called "$200 pencil." This well-known illustration speaks to the astounding accumulation of costs associated with the many transactions involved in acquiring and selling goods. Each transaction, from raising a purchase order through to generating payment, involves a different function in a company—accounting, finance, inventory, manufacturing, shipping, and so on. And each transaction has an associated cost. Yet each is an essential step in the activity of selling our pencil.

Since there are no functional redundancies to eliminate, companies look to automating trans-action systems in order to increase throughput and at the same time lower the cost per transaction. The same steps are being performed by the same

areas of the company. It just takes less time and costs less money.

But for all that automation has done to help perform transactions faster and more cheaply, the net impact has been relegated to a few functional areas and discrete operational processes. This has certainly been an important win for efficiency, but it is not the performance management end-game.

Today, with many operational processes automated, organizations are still left with a number of unanswered performance-defining questions. For example, how does a company know with certainty that its customers are satisfied? How does it know where the supply chain is breaking down? How does a company know it is building the right product? For the right market? And if it is not, how does it figure out what changes need to be made, and when?

The quick answer might be that if your product isn't selling, you go back to the drawing board and try again. However, if product development cycles and business planning cycles are out of sync, then success in finding the "right" product is left to little more than chance.

To remain competitive, companies must look beyond their tactical cycles. They must align business planning with business execution.

Organizations are making great strides toward aligning execution with strategic goals by auto-mating cross-functional enterprise processes, like customer relationship management (CRM) and supply chain management (SCM). Essentially a chain of interrelated functions, core processes like these are what ultimately drive value for a company.

While this new cross-functional focus has resulted in significant gains—faster customer acquisition, more consistent and responsive customer service, more efficient supply chain processes, and faster knowledge transfer—it is still ultimately about transactions, not performance.

The fundamental question remains unanswered. How is your company really *doing?*

In the same way that automation has allowed businesses to accelerate and enhance what they do operationally, companies can apply systems and technologies that do the same for how they operate strategically. By automating management processes, organizations can close the loop between strategy, planning, and execution.

Companies can accomplish this in two ways: by explicitly connecting managers and decision-makers at all levels of the organization to the business through information access and by connecting them to each other to improve their collective understanding of the principles and levers driving the business. In doing so, companies must reevaluate how they manage the strategic business cycles and processes most closely tied to business design: the planning, budgeting, and management of the business as a whole.

Today, businesses have process complexities to manage that were unheard of during the days of early automation. Companies operate within a web of value that connects suppliers and partners and customers. Mastering performance imperatives for the whole business means mastering the value chain.

Cross-Value-Chain Processes and Performance

From original equipment to raw materials to distribution, vertical integration epitomized the monopoly era of the early 1900s. Industrial titans like the Fords carved out their empires by owning every-thing from the smelting plants, to the automobile manufacturing plants, to the seat manu-

> **Making performance a key initiative within a company is difficult. The difficulty is compounded when you also have to manage performance outside your organization, across your value chain.**

facturing plants, to the engineering design shops, and even the sales offices.

In recent years, the business landscape has evolved from one of centralization to one of specialization, where key business processes are distributed across a value chain of discrete companies. Today, functional tasks such as human resources, purchasing, and information systems and technology are routinely outsourced to third-party suppliers. While these processes are essential to the functioning of any company, they aren't necessarily representative of the company's own core competencies.

Increasingly, we are seeing companies outsource business processes that reside significantly closer to their core value proposition. A common example of this occurrence is collaborative product development. Companies that manufacture personal computers, for instance, may outsource production of the casings to a strategic partner whose core competency is specifically in this area. This leaves the manufacturer free to concentrate its efforts on its own area of competence, that of designing and building the "guts"of the PC.

But rather than make life easier for a company, what this specialization has done is simply reinforce the interdependent nature of each component of the process, further highlighting

the need for each discrete operation to function as coherently as if it were a single entity. Operating in such a tightly integrated fashion is the new business imperative if companies are to achieve peak performance, particularly in the face of a significantly more competitive landscape, one that is increasingly global in scale.

Making performance a key initiative within a company is difficult. The difficulty is compounded when you also have to manage performance outside your organization, across your value chain. Both challenges require that companies value decision-makers as more than just "inputs" plugging into processes. They must create an environment where managers clearly own a component of overall performance. How this is done is the subject of the eight principles put forward in this book.

The Smart
and the Fast

Dell and Wal-Mart are companies whose business models epitomize efficiency and success. Once the stuff of science fiction, these case studies in innovation have redefined how companies compete within their respective industries. They include practices such as outsourcing components of the value chain like just-in-time shipping and manufacturing and high-speed, low-hassle e-commerce.

In choosing to make information readily accessible across their value chain and to distribute ownership of business performance to their partners, suppliers, and customers, companies such as these have done more than create a business model for the information age: they have established a business approach that cultivates innovation, rapid response to opportunity, and optimized performance. By continuing to nourish this strategy, these companies have remained consistently at the forefront of their industries in terms of marketability, profitability, and vision.

In today's increasingly global and internetworked business economy, competitive advantage ultimately comes down to the ability to generate new sources of value—over and over again. As companies become more broadly distributed across geographies, time zones, and corporate lines, one of the most vital qualities an organization can foster will be the innovation of its people and processes, anchored by a sound perception of the business and appropriate actions.

Innovation demands a different way of thinking: about how you connect employees so as to foster knowledge sharing and trust, about how you provide service to—and interact with—your customers, and about how you collaborate with suppliers and other key partners to seize new opportunities for value creation. And while innovation is often associated with inspiration, creativity, and flexibility, its real value is typically spelled out right on the balance sheet through new streams of revenue, reduced costs, and more efficient business processes.

The time to think about these issues is now. Turmoil and confusion in the marketplace have irrevocably changed the rules of engagement. In such a volatile environment, only the most agile and forward-thinking firms will survive.

Integration, in business, is about making the discrete assets of your company work together holistically: your data, your technology, and—most importantly—your people.

As organizations in industries worldwide confront the challenge of accelerating change, it is critical that we revisit first principles. We will do this by taking a bird's-eye view of two of the fundamental drivers for innovation: integration and collaboration. We will also examine how these basic requirements for long-term business success impact the way organizations manage their business.

The Importance of Integration in Business Today

When all key players who touch your value chain have a deep, holistic view into how that value chain is performing, they can weave a net of value that trolls the marketplace for new opportunities. But to create this net, all links in the value chain must be tightly interconnected.

Integration, in business, is about making the discrete assets of your company work together holistically: your data, your technology, and—most importantly—your people.

But beyond making business processes more efficient, integration is increasingly becoming an essential business requirement for driving innovation and value creation. As Dell and Wal-Mart illustrate, the seamless integration of employees, suppliers, and customers has become a critical factor for success in each of these categories. The simple fact is that the more broadly distributed your company becomes, the greater the need to have a shared perspective on the goals, expectations, and performance of the business and to integrate your systems and your people. If they are not integrated, the performance of the business cannot be controlled and, in most cases, it cannot even be tracked.

According to Michael Hammer and Andersen Consulting, we are in the era of the "collaborative economy."[1] Likewise, Morgan Stanley Dean Witter has proclaimed this the age of "collaborative commerce."[2] However we choose to describe it, this emerging trend toward integration is distinct from past eras. For one thing, it has changed the nature of competition. In the past, competitors tended to have a much clearer picture of who the enemy was. As such, they could focus their efforts on wrestling market share from whichever competitor posed the greatest threat. And generally, it was the biggest company—the one that controlled its suppliers and manufacturers—that would "win." The problem

these days, however, is that it is getting increasingly difficult to distinguish who the enemy is. In fact, it is quite common to find companies that were once competitors looking for ways to work together to service a common customer. Conventional wisdom has proven that competitiveness is no longer dependent upon sheer brute force. Today, competitive advantage depends largely on the efficiency and effectiveness—the integration—of a company's value chain.[3]

Collaboration: The People Side of Integration

Collaboration is all about people agreeing to work together in a *de facto* manner in order to set and achieve common goals. It enables people and organizations to draw maximum value and knowledge out of every relevant information source. For companies to succeed in an interdependent business environment, collaboration—like integration—must occur at every level of the company.

Collaboration and integration must go hand in hand if companies are to exploit the full

> **Collaboration and integration must go hand in hand if companies are to exploit the full potential of their people and processes.**

potential of their people and processes. Collaboration requires an integrated view of the world, a shared context for understanding how a business functions and why. And integration is only as valuable as people's willingness to build collaborative relationships. When we analyze the noise of the marketplace over the past year or so, and looking forward several years, business survival has become—and will continue to be—increasingly dependent on a shared perspective, integration, and collaboration.

These business imperatives, in turn, make performance management more fundamental to corporate strategy than ever before.

The Performance Imperative

So far, we've seen that by integrating people and systems, and by fostering collaboration, companies can maximize performance. But how exactly are we defining performance? Performance is the intended outcome of a business process, be it a transactional process such as purchasing, a marketing process such as lead generation, or processes related to the development, manufacturing, and delivery of products and services.

Given that each business process is an activity—or a group of activities—conducted by one or more business functions, we can conclude that performance is simply the cumulative and collective effect of decision-making over time. In other words, the people managing the business processes—and making decisions—across all levels of the company and across the value chain have a cumulative impact on how well the company strategy is fulfilled.

Not surprisingly, the combined weight of these many decisions can have a direct impact on a company's success or failure. Thus, if decision-makers in an organization understand only their small piece of the business pie—if they do not

have a common understanding of the company's overall goals and priorities—then that organization cannot hope to advance its competitive advantage.

Instead of managing performance, these individuals are simply measuring processes.

But when everyone understands how to manage

Thus, if decision-makers in an organization understand only their small piece of the business pie—if they do not have a common understanding of the company's overall goals and priorities—then that organization cannot hope to advance its competitive advantage.

their part of the business—and is empowered to do it—you make the quantum leap from simply experiencing or measuring business results to actually controlling outcomes. As a result, companies can make the shift from simply having visibility into process performance to actually steering the performance of the business as a whole.

As corporate agility becomes the overriding imperative for success in such a turbulent economy, companies must reconsider the importance of all decision-makers as owners of business performance—from executives to line-of-business managers and knowledge workers.

[1] From "The Dawn of the Collaborative Economy: Building Strategies and Operational Alliances with the Internet," October 12-13, 2000, Boston, Massachusetts, hosted by Michael Hammer, Ph.D., and Andersen Consulting.

[2] From Charles Phillips and Mary Meeker, "The B2B Internet Report: Collaborative Commerce," Morgan Stanley Dean Witter Equity Research North America, April 2000.

[3] "Value chain" refers simply to the chain of businesses and people linked together to create value for your customers, from the customers themselves back to the original manufacturers. Value chains can be exceptionally complex or very simple.

BUSINESS PERFORMANCE FACTS

In early 2001, Cognos Incorporated commissioned an independent study on performance management and decision-making. More than 400 companies with revenues between $100 million and $1 billion responded to a series of questions about how the rise of internetworked business processes was affecting the performance of their business. The results revealed the following insights:

1

Performance management is everyone's responsibility—but few decision-makers understand how their decisions impact company performance.

- Less than 60% of companies surveyed said they had a standard process for measuring company performance against preset targets.

- Line-of-business managers are largely responsible for measuring performance, followed most closely by the board of directors or senior management team, and directors. And yet, only one in two managers indicated they had a clear sense of how their department's performance impacts the company overall. Only 30% said they clearly understood their key performance drivers.

- Nearly two-thirds of those surveyed (63%) said their company had an explicit vision or mission statement. But only 66% of those said they track performance back to those statements.

2

When it comes to performance management, every decision-maker counts— including decision-makers in partner and customer companies.

- For the majority of companies, there is no definitive management level at which key decisions affecting performance are made. Rather, these decisions are made at many different levels in different companies, across all functions.

- Customers and partners are the two groups that most companies are willing to share both performance information and transaction data with. Fully half (50%) of larger companies surveyed said they share this information with both customers and partners.

3

The barriers to performance-focused decision-making are largely cultural.

- A company's culture is more likely than anything else to be a barrier. The greatest barriers to increasing information access were stated as:
  - Cultural mistrust of information sharing
  - Cultural resistance to change

- Decisions-by-committee, lack of collaboration, and insufficient time were said to hinder decision-making the most. Other significant impediments to successful decision-making included:
  - Cultural tendency within the company to hoard information
  - Lack of empowerment to make decisions at the point of greatest impact

4

People are looking for technological solutions to these challenges.

- While a variety of tools and processes are available to decision-makers as they gather information, most said they relied on their own experience and instinct to guide them, as well as input from colleagues and direct reports.

- Fewer than 35% of decision-makers said they currently use their own corporate data—via electronic reports or analysis tools—to inform decisions, but nearly 60% indicated they were counting on technology to enable faster decision-making and increase the coordination between decision-makers over the next five years.

(Source: Independently commissioned survey, March 2001. Copyright © Cognos Incorporated.)

Principles of
High-Performance
Business

A high-performance company works, in many ways, like a high-performance yacht: a balance of innovative design, agility, and speed. Wind conditions, like market conditions, are continuously monitored, with each shift demanding instantaneous response. Collaboration—between navigator and helmsman, captain and crew—is seamless and focused on achieving a single outcome: to win the race. Each task is fully integrated and coordinated across the vessel and by team members ashore, so as to realize maximum impact. Every decision—to trim the sails or grind the winches—is immediate and informed, hardwired into the systems and processes that impel the yacht forward. Performance is precisely measured, from sail to superstructure. But above all, a high-performance yacht is driven by information: a combination of knowledge and experience that informs the decisions that result in victory.

Enlist Everyone

Don't Lock Down— Link Up

Empower at the Point of Impact

Build Your Truth

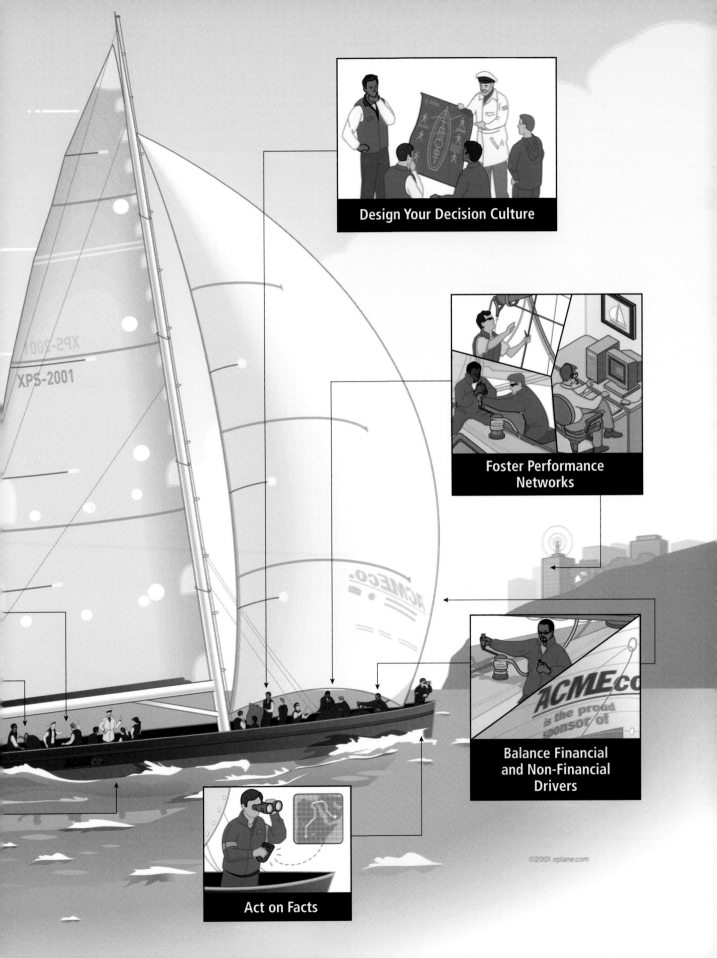

Design Your Decision Culture

Foster Performance Networks

Balance Financial and Non-Financial Drivers

Act on Facts

©2006 xplane.com

The role of every decision-maker in a high-performance business is to understand how effectively the business is performing and why it's performing that way—and then to make decisions that drive success. But how do companies facilitate this degree of empowerment? In this section, we will define what the high-performance business looks like and outline the principles and mind-shifts that need to take place in order to get there.

HIGH-PERFORMANCE PEOPLE

The fundamental driver of any business is its people. However, if a company is to maximize its effectiveness, people need to be able to work in an environment that supports what makes them effective; otherwise, the company is leaving its value potential on the table. This means substantiating "our people are our best asset" rhetoric. But how is this actually done? In this section, we'll look at practical ways to enlist and arm your people and, by doing so, create a foundation for collaboration and innovation that enables a high-performance business.

PRINCIPLE 1 | ENLIST EVERYONE

Every crew member is engaged to identify new opportunities for maximizing performance and to respond to challenges that could hinder it. Every role is clearly articulated to ensure that each decision reflects how each crew member's role impacts the performance of the yacht overall.

Decision-makers—at all levels—must have a shared, validated, and holistic view into the company's overall strategy, a view that clarifies and articulates how their individual roles impact overall performance.

Managers outside of the finance department have direct accountability for virtually 100 % of the business. Most are not senior-level decision-makers; rather, they are line managers, mid-level decision-makers, and knowledge or frontline workers. While these individuals typically have the most in-depth understanding of the numbers within their sphere of responsibility, they also tend to have limited insight into their company's strategic objectives. Creating a high-performance enterprise requires that all employees have a shared, validated, and holistic view into the company's overall strategy— and a clear understanding of how their individual roles impact overall performance.

In the 1980s, leading exponents of business process reengineering—Michael Hammer, most notably— argued that flattening the organization was the key to giving management greater visibility into business performance. And it was the key to increasing the effectiveness of line-of-business workers by empowering them to make decisions about their area of accountability. The ultimate goal of reengineering was to cut costs and improve process efficiency.

In their 1996 book *The Balanced Scorecard,* Robert S. Kaplan and David P. Norton took this goal a step further by focusing on how to give senior management a broader view into the business, but from more than just a financial perspective. Their goal was to improve the drivers of business performance in order to provide a better, faster, more streamlined value proposition to customers.

But to truly fulfill the promise of a high-performance business, companies today must focus on the impact of all decision-makers across the entire value chain, including those within the organization and those external to the company who co-own strategic processes, such as supply chain and distribution.

The Decision Collective

The leveling of the organization rooted in the business process reengineering and corporate reengineering movements of the 1980s continues to take place even today— in fact, it is accelerating. We are already seeing the repercussions of this shift as the capacity for decision-making, formerly reserved for the most senior people in the company, is of necessity passed down and across the organization.

High-performance companies recognize that everyone is part of the decision collective and, as such, work hard to ensure their people are empowered to make and execute the decisions that drive the business forward.

The speed and effectiveness with which people make and execute a decision is a locus of any company's competitive advantage today. High-performance companies recognize that everyone is part of the decision collective and, as such, work hard to ensure their people are empowered to make and execute the decisions that drive the business forward.

Products may come and go. Markets may evolve. But businesses that nurture an informed, collaborative decision culture, particularly in the midst of change, are those that will generate sustainable competitive advantage. They will operate their businesses more efficiently than their competitors. In addition, they will be positioned to tap into new sources of value and seize new opportunities that arise out of deeper insight and empowerment on the part of informed managers and other decision-makers.

LAYING THE FOUNDATION

Invest in Business Knowledge

A company's competitive advantage can be sustained only when managers view their activities—and the financial allocations that fund them—as an investment in the company's future. Because these financial allocations or budgets are the financial expression of a company's strategy, decision-makers need to view budget planning as an opportunity to review the levers they have at hand to execute the company's goals. Viewing the budgeting process as an investment process, rather than as a compliance exercise, is vital. To create this kind of mindset, companies must invest in their people's understanding of:

- Their area's role within the extended enterprise
- Their area's impact on non-financial performance drivers such as products and customers

- Their area's contribution to high-level performance indicators such as profitability

Successfully enlisting everyone in a high-velocity, high-impact performance management environment such as this necessitates that everyone be schooled on how to use information most appropriately. More than any other factor, these practices influence the success of a company's ability to manage performance.

Identify Key Performance Management Roles and Resources

Enlisting everyone means identifying the key skills and roles required to successfully execute your performance management strategy. In addition to engaging executive and management support, companies must consider the impact of employees whose roles traverse multiple functions, as it is these

> **"We really try to live by the principle of enlisting everyone as an advocate of business performance."**
>
> Gary Loveman, Chief Operating Officer, Harrah's Entertainment, Inc.

individuals who typically have the detailed focus and understanding necessary to complement management's higher level business focus.

PRINCIPLE IN ACTION

Harrah's Entertainment, Inc. is one of the largest casino-entertainment companies in the United States.

Harrah's recently won a number of awards for technology and innovation—an occurrence which might seem unusual for a 64-year-old company. Part of the reason for this was the company's introduction three years ago of a meritocratic environment.

Gary Loveman, Chief Operating Officer, describes how his $3 billion company has focused on the credo that "the quality of the idea carries the day, not the stature of its advocate."

"We really try to live by the principle of enlisting everyone as an advocate of business performance," says Loveman. "There is no project that's my pet project or the chairman's pet project. It's a matter of using analysis to debate the merits of whatever concepts we think have the greatest efficacy. That has fuelled an awful lot of well-intentioned and powerful innovation.

"We structured all of this work, in customer relationship management in particular, using a classical statistician's approach. We are constantly testing, learning, and retesting, in a business that is fortunately a high-frequency purchase business. This enables us to get feedback from our hypothesis quickly and incorporate that into what we do next time."

For Harrah's, this practice goes right down into the operating levels of all of the casino businesses, feeding into all principal marketing engines throughout the company. The information access and analysis tools they use to support this initiative are used daily in all the 25 operating businesses.

According to Loveman, "That places the power of innovation in the hands of people who are out there engaging our guests and creating the environment in which our guests enjoy our facilities."

PRINCIPLE 2 | DON'T LOCK DOWN—LINK UP

Interconnections between every crew member are solidified to ensure a common understanding of objectives and a seamless exchange of knowledge for informed decision-making.

Solidify the interconnections, relationships, and shared goals between the decision-makers who co-own specific areas of business performance—at every layer of the business: technological, cultural, and commercial.

To avoid pitfalls like inefficiency, isolation, and tentative execution, companies must focus on solidifying the interconnections, relationships, and shared goals between the decision-makers who co-own specific areas of business performance—at every layer of the business: technological, cultural, and commercial.

The Manager's Dilemma

The manager's dilemma is this: "How do I ensure that the people below me are making sound decisions without becoming a control freak or a roadblock to efficiency?"

The standard response to this dilemma is to lock down the business by reorganizing, bottlenecking decisions, insisting on committee-based decision-making, withholding information, and initiating a host of other "back-to-basics" strategies. However, business performance is systemic. Trying to revitalize a business by focusing almost exclusively on its organizational structure is tantamount to putting it on life support: the systems may be functional, but is the business really still alive?

The key to building an organic business performance management system is to understand and counteract the "manager's dilemma."

Issuing orders does little to resolve the question of disconnectedness. The real solution lies in connecting people—to the business and to each other. The role of technology in this undertaking is pivotal. Individual technologies will feed effective decision-making, but a holistic, integrated performance-support infrastructure creates effective companies. However, this kind of solution will work only if you focus on linking up your assets rather than locking them down.

Effective organizations no longer allow individual departments or geographically dispersed branch operations to deploy incompatible computer systems. They understand that no matter what the task or where it is performed, everybody still works for the same company. Whether it is managing customer relationships, successfully marketing products, or simply getting things done, intercompany systems must be capable of speaking to one another. Too often, however, companies abandon their decision-makers to a wilderness of inconsistent data, leaving them without a clue as to how the company expects them

> **Issuing orders does little to resolve the question of disconnectedness. The real solution lies in connecting people—to the business and to each other.**

to understand or interpret this data—let alone collaborate with other decision-makers.

To push decision-making out across the organization—and even further across the value chain to suppliers, partners, and customers—the first imperative is to create an infrastructure that can support it, centralize it, and ensure that everyone is working with the same information and rules for using it. This is a basic requirement for linking up, rather than locking down.

LAYING THE FOUNDATION

Appoint a Metrics Master

Performance metrics such as product performance, customer satisfaction, and cost allocations often break down when rolled up (aggregated), down (de-aggregated), and across different functions. In other words, as soon as anyone attempts to correlate metrics between different business units or across more multiple levels of management, these metrics tend to become inaccurate or quickly misunderstood—for the simple reason that the way one person measures success can be very different from how someone else does. What companies are only now realizing is that agility, efficiency, and innovation are born precisely from this intersection of metrics.

To counter broken-metric syndrome, companies must set in place a process for rolling out metrics that are in sync with a company's core objectives and specify a metrics master who works with all levels of management to ensure the integrity of these metrics as accurate indicators of company performance.

Invest in Information Knowledge

In recent years, companies have come to realize that while the technical sophistication of their employees is more ubiquitous than ever before, resistance to change—in all aspects of the business—is still the cultural norm. This creates an entirely new series of challenges for business. From the perspective of decision-making, reporting software, paper reports, and analysis tools are too often wasted because many decision-makers don't fully understand how to exploit the information at their disposal.

Companies can facilitate change by investing in education and by teaching people how to use information—for example, providing courses that explain how to use and manipulate data. At the same time, companies can reinforce change momentum by challenging decision-makers, making it their responsibility to interpret data appropriately. Together, these investments counter-act the manager's dilemma discussed earlier.

Color the Gray Areas

Silos are the result of gray areas in the definitions of roles and responsibilities for departments, teams, and individuals. If a company is to remove these gray areas and rally around performance management, a fundamental mind-shift needs to happen. Companies like NCR, and Harrah's are restructuring their internal teams to ensure that every information asset is linked up—including their people. In doing so, these companies are removing the gray areas that create informational and functional silos.

PRINCIPLE IN ACTION

NCR Corporation is a $5 billion global enterprise that provides Relationship Technology™ solutions to customers around the world. The company's business solutions include the Teradata® database and analytical applications such as customer relationship management (CRM) and demand chain management, store automation systems, and automated teller machines (ATMs).

In the mid-'90s, NCR overhauled its existing corporate strategy, moving from a regional-centric and product-focused approach to a solutions-based approach driven by the needs of the customer.

For NCR, changing its business model also meant a change in the information needs of its 33,000 employees spread out over 100 countries. Local operations had to broaden their focus to ensure a much more integrated view of the business across discrete functions as well as geography. Information became a critical requirement to reinforce consistent worldwide operating processes and, ultimately, to drive process improvements. This requirement also necessitated standardized performance measures and tracking across the business. By making a concerted effort to link formerly heterogeneous offices and information technologies together as a single, global entity—including a complete overhaul of its data warehousing systems—NCR was able to connect both geographic and functional islands of knowledge while removing barriers to efficiency.

Gaining a single holistic view of the business—one that accurately reflects the company's overall corporate strategy—has had a tremendous impact on NCR's performance. Mark Hurd, president of NCR Corporation and Chief Operating Officer, Teradata Division, picks up the story: "For example, 'mean time to repair' was a key customer service metric that was being applied inconsistently—if at all—throughout the company. As a result, it was extremely difficult for us to ensure a coordinated, globally consistent approach to improving the performance of that metric, and thus the performance of our business overall."

To remedy the issue, being a technology company, NCR built a data warehouse and created a common definition of the measurement, with a corresponding business rule that would be applied by all managers. In doing so, NCR enabled managers not only to measure their repair times in the same way across the organization, but also to compare where best practices are occurring and identify areas where they're not.

> **"Today, nearly every customer service team around the world views this performance measure the same way— and at every level of management."**
>
> Mark Hurd, President, NCR Corporation, and Chief Operating Officer, Teradata Division

"Today," says Hurd, "nearly every customer service team around the world views this performance measure the same way—and at every level of management. More importantly, our *NCR@Your Service* solution now lets NCR customers view their own service contract details and equipment maintenance online."

NCR's effort to interconnect its people has paid off handsomely. It has made it easier for decision-makers to identify and analyze problems while uncovering new opportunities to improve performance. NCR's customer service department alone has saved $3 to $4 million a year by automating service-level agreement reporting to customers.

PRINCIPLE 3 | EMPOWER AT THE POINT OF IMPACT

Every crew member is empowered to make the decisions appropriate to their role—decisions deemed necessary to accelerate performance. Armed with the tools and information to make informed decisions, every crew member is made accountable.

The decisions each employee makes must be appropriate to their role as a decision-maker. Accountability and empowerment must be cultivated at all levels.

In a high-performance organization, individuals know whether the decision they are making is appropriate to their role as a decision-maker. They also know who should be making the decision, and they make it easy for that person to do their job.

Decisions Float

It is a fundamental law of the physics of business that decisions will float up to wherever a person is authorized to make a call on an issue. This is the decision point. If people are not empowered to make decisions, then decision-making will be delegated up the chain of command. This upward delegation forces senior decision-makers to make decisions that aren't appropriate to their scope of impact. Clearly, a CEO should not be making decisions about the color of a product's packaging, the wording of an advertisement, or the number of widgets needed to build a certain product.

The counterforce to "floating decisions" is co-ordinated, distributed decision-making, where the person closest to the point of impact for a particular decision also owns the decision point. Approval for the execution of a decision should happen as close to this point as possible, with minimal upward delegation. Distributing *de facto* decision-making power to the decision-maker who is closest to the decision's outcome acts like gravity for decisions, keeping them attached to the point of greatest impact, and thereby accelerating the speed of decision-making.

LAYING THE FOUNDATION

Collaborate Around Decisions, Not Data

Collaboration is not about "decision-by-committee." It is not about consensus. Instead, it is about ensuring that people across your value chain share the same facts, context, and rationale for decision-making. Recommendations and decisions are easier to validate and can be communicated immediately across the network when consistent data is being fed to decision-makers. Business execution thus becomes faster and more precise.

But to realize the goal of distributed decision-making, decision-makers first need factual support for their decision—support that can be easily disseminated to other decision-makers across the network, as reports, data cubes, and other types of information.

Secondly, decision-makers must be able to articulate not only quantitative data, but also more qualitative information

> **Distributing *de facto* decision-making power to the decision-maker who is closest to the decision's outcome acts like gravity for decisions, keeping them attached to the point of greatest impact, and thereby accelerating the speed of decision-making.**

such as gut instinct or past experience. This might take the form of posting facts and opinions onto a secure intranet or extranet portal or transmitting information to other decision-makers via e-mail.

This functionality is a key enabler of collaboration. It means that decision-makers across the value chain can literally plug into a fellow employee's decision-making processes and anticipate the impact and repercussions of each decision. The alternative—upending a decision after it has been made or, worse, going back to the drawing board—is no longer viable in today's lean business environment.

The key is to ensure that everybody shares not only the same basic data but also the context by which this data is understood. In doing so, appropriate decisions can be made that are instantly valuable across the decision chain—decisions that can be instantly validated by other decision-makers because they share the same context.

Build Trust

One of the most significant obstacles to achieving distributed decision-making is the difficulty for managers to trust other people to make the right decision, for the right reasons, based on the right information, at the right time. Contrary to popular opinion, trust is not a prerequisite of collaboration. Rather, trust is born of demonstrated success and shared context. Decision-makers within an organization operate most effectively when they have an immediate, intuitive understanding of a person's rationale for making a decision. This shared validation is based on shared context over time and is a primary benefit of enabled information sharing. The link between trust, shared information, and context is critical. Trust emerges when decisions are made and then repeatedly validated by others. Validation is possible only when people are working from a shared context. In fact, having a shared context is a much more powerful (and less intensive) validation tool than personal justification after the fact. Once decision-makers are hardwired into the network, trust builds over time—trust in the system itself and trust in the effectiveness of those within the system. The result is accelerated, appropriate decision-making.

Understand the Anatomy of a Decision

While most people acknowledge decision-making as a key part of their job, the processes by which they actually make decisions are highly varied. Most do not operate under a strict decision-making protocol. Many senior managers assert that they make very few real decisions on a day-to-day basis. Instead, they receive recommendations from their direct reports, which they review with other senior decision-makers to ultimately create policies, strategies, and plans. They do not tend to see these processes as decisions but simply as the outward expression of a leadership position within a corporation.

> **It is critical that decision-makers are making decisions and dealing with information that is appropriate to their decision role. In other words, they should be making decisions that map to their point of impact on the company.**

And yet all of these—the recommendations, plans, decisions, and actions—are critical "decision-point" events in the decision-making process. Some may lead to other decisions while others lead to action. Regardless of what form a decision ultimately takes, it is critical that decision-makers are making decisions and dealing with information that is appropriate to their decision role. In other words, they should be making decisions that map to their point of impact on the company. In the same way that the production line manager would not be making decisions about the company's product vision, the vice president of marketing should not be dealing with the nuts and bolts of production line information.

And as different types of decisions should map to the decision-maker's breadth of influence, so too should the information that feeds a decision match the type of decision they are making. For example, a production line manager will typically

require information that is more tactical—i.e., data-intensive, less aggregated, and closer to the transaction details—than a CIO.

Information can be viewed or acted upon differently from decision-maker to decision-maker, particularly at different hierarchical levels within a company or across the value chain. The difference lies in the ratio of data to context, or what we refer to as the "information scope." Useful "information" always comprises both "data" and "context." Generally speaking, as you move higher up in an organization, context becomes a larger percentage

Rather than focusing on how much information they need, decision-makers should focus on the level and quality of information feeding their work.

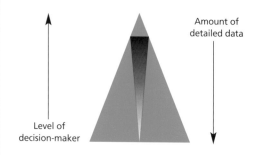

Inside each pyramid is an inverted pyramid representing the percent of business information that is accounted for. In the first pyramid the high-level decision-maker gets all the information available, but less detail, whereas in the second pyramid nobody gets all of the information available, and everyone is overwhelmed with detail.

Amount of detailed data

Level of decision-maker

Level of decision-maker

Amount of detailed data

This model is focused on the SCOPE of information.

This model is focused on the AMOUNT of information.

of the information feeding your decision. At the same time, transaction-level data that makes up the business at the broadest, lowest level becomes increasingly abstract.

Rather than focusing on how much information they need, decision-makers should focus on the level and quality of information feeding their work. Everything else can then be pushed aside. Decision-makers must ask themselves whether the information they are accumulating best reflects the types of decisions they need to make on a regular basis. Should it be more detailed, or more highly aggregated? What is motivating them to attend meetings or participate in the projects of those working under them? Decision-makers must focus on information that matches the scope of the decision they are making and ensure that the decision is being made at the point where it will have the most and best impact.

PRINCIPLE IN ACTION

Schneider Logistics is a leading provider of technology-based logistics services that effectively manage the flow of material, information, and funds through its customers' supply chains.

According to Bill Braddy, Vice President of Engineering and Knowledge Services, one of the key challenges facing Schneider was the length of time it took to respond to customer queries. Typically, a business analyst would contact

someone in Schneider's IT department in order to run queries on a variety of logistical scenarios such as "why are the costs of transportation on these lanes rising over the last quarter?" The outcome, however, would be what Braddy calls a "circular dance" in which each question would elicit a new question, causing a back-and-forth spiral that could ultimately take days to resolve. Today, Schneider is delivering information straight to its customers via the Web, reducing the time and resources required to solve complex problems. Alone, or by collaborating with a Schneider representative over the phone, customers can interact directly with the data themselves, thereby reducing query time to a matter of minutes.

> **"We brought the tools and information to the customer—to the point of impact—which lets them answer complex questions fast and make appropriate decisions about their business most efficiently for the simple reason that they—not our IT department—are best suited to do that."**
>
> Bill Braddy, Vice President of Engineering and Knowledge Services, Schneider Logistics

Says Braddy, "We brought the tools and information to the customer—to the point of impact—which lets them answer complex questions fast and make appropriate decisions about their business most efficiently for the simple reason that they—not our IT department—are best suited to do that."

HIGH-PERFORMANCE PRACTICES

The previous section described how companies foster high-performance people by enabling them to become self-informed, make more effective decisions, and collaborate with each other in order to maximize a company's overall performance. But the business environment within which your people are placed—the environment created by your most fundamental business practices—can either make people successful or stand in their way.

In this section, we examine the approaches companies must take to establish an environment that cultivates high-impact decision-makers. These are the principles for building high-performance practices.

PRINCIPLE 4 | BUILD YOUR TRUTH

Each decision made by a crew member is driven by a shared understanding of purpose, one that clearly defines the impact of that decision on the yacht's performance while ensuring performance goals are consistently communicated and realized.

Every decision must be based on a shared "truth," a framework of shared understanding that clearly defines the impact of each decision on the company's performance while ensuring performance goals are consistently communicated and realized.

A commitment to high-performance decision-making means that all decision-makers agree to found their decisions based on a shared "truth." This shared truth must exist in order for decision-makers to understand their own impact on the company's performance and to ensure performance goals are consistently communicated and realized.

For a business, truth is the contract by which people agree to interpret, use, and respond to information. It is the shared context by which decision-makers collectively agree to understand the data, the events, and the challenges they face every day. This context is fed by a clear corporate vision and mandate. It is also physically instantiated into an organization's information infrastructure. In this way, a company's technical backbone can parallel its goals and its culture.

"Measure what is measurable, and make measurable what is not so." —Galileo Galilei

What Is Your Truth?

Before Copernicus and Galileo arrived on the scene in the 16th and 17th centuries, conventional wisdom held that the earth was at the center of the universe and that everything in the heavens orbited it. For the average Westerner, this was the truth. It was fact, *painstakingly, scientifically researched fact* supported by the ultimate source of truth at the time: the church.

In the centuries that have followed, we have come to see the universe in a completely different way: as a series of galaxies and solar systems that orbit stars or as a massive energy center through which fields of quantum energy, particles, anti-particles, and a host of other invisible forces flow. Every day, these facts are substantiated and reinforced by scientific research.

What changed to enable this new way of seeing things? Simply, we evolved a new *context* by which to collectively understand the universe. At the time of Copernicus and Galileo, the official view of the universe was that it was created expressly for man; thus, man naturally resided at its center. The ongoing secularization of the sciences, and of society in general, has created new contexts that have, in turn, enabled new truths. But who is to say that our truth will not one day seem simplistic and naïve, or simply wrong?

> **Although data is important, it should not be equated with truth or exactness by virtue of the simple fact that it is data. Fact and truth reflect the context by which you understand the information at hand.**

Truth is never absolute. And this is especially true in business. It seems like a simplistic statement, yet it is one that must be revisited in the information age—an age where "truth" and "data" are often equated. Although data is important, it should not be equated with truth or exactness by virtue of the simple fact that it is data. Fact and truth reflect the context by which you understand the information at hand. And when it comes to managing business performance, understanding the facts—having a "true" perspective on the business—is judged by how certain you are that the right person is measuring the right things at the right time.

A commitment to building a high-performance business demands that all of us recognize this distinction and agree to shape a shared view of "truth." The key to achieving this, however, is that all decision-makers buy into this common view of truth or at least be able to defend their decisions against it. By doing so, decision-makers can better understand their own relevance and contribution to the company while ensuring that performance goals remain consistent across the value chain.

LAYING THE FOUNDATION

Develop Your Truth Contract

You have enlisted the right people for the right jobs. Now you need to identify the context within which they should operate. A context that reflects not only the fundamental goals established by the senior management team, but also:

- First and foremost: a top-down declaration of the commitment to being a high-performance company
- Key strategies for meeting these goals
- The factors that drive success or failure in meeting these goals
- The levers that decision-makers can use to steer the company toward the goals
- A system for measuring the company's effectiveness in meeting these goals

- A process for guiding people out of the old truth and into the new

Once this has been achieved, the rest of the organization must then become involved. The truth needs to be distributed, and decision-makers need to understand how their jobs should operate within this shared context. This means identifying the following:

1. The actual operational processes that drive company performance, and the decision points that reside across these processes
2. The metrics each decision-maker is accountable for:
   - Financial objectives—the "numbers": financial goals, output goals, key standardized calculations such as profitability and productivity, to ensure a common reference point
   - Qualitative objectives—metrics and measurement systems for less tangible factors that impact business: customer satisfaction, employee satisfaction, the health of your partnerships, etc.
3. The feedback process and its owner
4. The escalation point

PRINCIPLE IN ACTION

The worldwide market for window coverings and architectural products is fiercely competitive. Margins for error are slim. For Hunter Douglas, a $1.4 billion global enterprise, success to date has been largely the result of the company's performance-oriented management style of "maximum accountability and minimum interference."

In such a competitive industry, safeguarding strategic information about the company as a whole is a key priority. As a result, the company's management style also ensures that visibility into goals and responsibility for managing performance are limited to a manager's specific area of accountability. This structure, according to Gordon Khan, Senior Vice President and Chief Financial Officer of Hunter Douglas' North American operations, created a number of challenges when trying to assess and maximize performance for the company.

Because the company is so highly decentralized, many general managers view their individual divisions as near-autonomous companies and, as such, do their own thing. Until recently, this included managing the way they measured and reported on performance. "Everybody would talk differently about what their numbers meant and how they defined various metrics." While this may have been fine for each division, considerable time and effort needed to be expended to get a solid understanding of how the company was performing overall. After consolidating and adjusting each division's numbers into a manageable—and understandable—whole, little time would be left for analysis and planning. The ability of management to make critical performance decisions when and where it mattered most was severely compromised.

Says Khan, "When I joined the company, I made it a top priority to streamline the process so we could spend more time assessing business performance and less time preparing the information." Khan exploited the threat of Y2K to begin the task of creating a shared context by which every division collectively viewed and understood its data. Key to this was the need to standardize 16 different general ledgers into one company-wide financial reporting perspective, and the establishment of common metrics by which to map performance to the company's overall objectives. "Our CEO decreed that to facilitate how we manage business performance across the board, North American managers must present their pieces of the business according to this common view."

The strategy worked. By aligning all managers to work from a "common truth," Hunter Douglas North America is establishing new performance benchmarks for the company's global operations. "Today, we're all talking about the same numbers," explains Khan. "By implementing a common framework of understanding, each division now speaks a common language. Every chart is identical to the next guy's chart. We don't have to decipher individual metrics. We don't have to second-guess the decisions or the performance criteria upon which each decision is based. We can trust the information presented to us, implicitly. We know what to look for. And, ultimately, because our information is now framed within a common context, we can gain critical insights into the performance of our business more effectively than ever before."

PRINCIPLE 5 | ACT ON FACTS

Wind speed. Currents. Distance to market. To make and act on informed, effective decisions, each crew member must have access to, and a clear understanding of the facts that impact performance.

When people feel they understand the facts and have the validation they need to act, they can make informed, effective decisions that drive high-impact business performance.

The ultimate goal of decision-making is to achieve an effective outcome. When people feel they understand the facts and have the validation they need to act, they can make informed, effective decisions that drive high-impact business performance.

People have a love–hate relationship with data. On the one hand, there is a fundamental mistrust of it. Human error, individual agendas, and the ease with which data can be misconstrued and manipulated all feed this mistrust. On the other hand, there is a tendency to appeal to data as "truth" simply because it is a point of data. But in the end, data is relevant only if it is accurate and useful. And it is useful only if business people can apply it to decisions that lead to effective action.

Typically, the most vital source of information about your business is contained in the stores of data held within a company's databases, data marts, and data warehouses. However, only when business rules and other "contextualizers" have been applied to this data does an organization have the real facts that are pivotal for both your company and your decision-making processes. Having access to this information is the first step to making an effective decision.

The problem many organizations face today, however, is people's inability to process the sheer volume of information at their fingertips. This often forces managers to revert to making decisions based on instinct or anecdotal evidence—or worse yet, to postpone decisions. In order to escape "instinct-based" decision-making or analysis paralysis, decision-makers need to have high-value, low-volume information that is directly relevant to their activities and, more importantly, provided to them at key times, such as:

- On a regular, ongoing basis
- Whenever they want to look into a particular area of the business
- When important opportunities and problems arise

Having access to specific information at these critical pulse-points helps decision-makers process information faster, react more quickly and effectively to changing business conditions, and better drive performance.

But acting fast isn't just about making decisions quickly; it's also about how quickly your decision can be validated by other stakeholders. Only by linking up, collaborating, and building your truth can you establish a cultural framework for clear and consistent validation. Once you share this common foundation, and build an information infrastructure to support it, the facts become your quickest path to impact.

> **Only when business rules and other "contextualizers" have been applied to this data does an organization have the real facts that are pivotal for both your company and your decision-making processes. Having access to this information is the first step to making an effective decision.**

LAYING THE FOUNDATION

Focus on High-Value, Low-Volume Information

In order to enact this principle, companies must focus on high-value, low-volume information. Typically, this information is:

- Based primarily on empirical data or fact
- Directly related to the decision-maker's activities or scope of influence, across all the potential combinations that this entails
- Packaged in a way that matches the way they think and enables them to get at the details when they are needed
- Highly prioritized (e.g., "The three most important factors affecting a given situation are….")

The distinction between high-value, low-volume information and what is commonly perceived as "data" is much like the difference between a newspaper and a phone book. Both provide valuable information, but while the newspaper tells you what you need to know (and is often delivered right to your door), the phone book requires that you know what you're looking for and how to go about getting it. One way to think about high-value, low-volume information is to visualize information "sweet spots." On a golf club, the sweet spot is the point where the energy from the swinging club is most effectively transferred to the ball. If you miss the sweet spot, you get less distance and less accuracy. If you hit the sweet spot right, the ball will take off—even if you hit it with less velocity. The same analogy can be applied to information. The most valuable information for corporate decision-making is concentrated in a relatively small number of sweet spots. These sweet spots represent the intersection of key dimensions of information (such as customer, product, location) that are most useful in tracking the performance of the business in a given area. By understanding these sweet spots—what they are and where they reside—

> **The most valuable information for corporate decision-making is concentrated in a relatively small number of sweet spots. These sweet spots represent the intersection of key dimensions of information (such as customer, product, location) that are most useful in tracking the performance of the business in a given area.**

decision-makers are able to track, analyze, and then use data to drive up production, drive down costs, and drive the business toward a more performance-centric model. Sweet spots underscore the importance of quality over quantity when it comes to information. And since sweet spots are most closely associated with key activities performed by management at all levels, managers receive only those chunks of information that help them react faster and more efficiently to changing business conditions. Furthermore, the key performance indicators that make up these sweet spots also tend to drive the associated line items in financial statements. This practice creates high-performance managers who oversee discrete universes of critical success factors at high-leverage points across the value chain. The difficulty of working with this high-leverage information is largely eliminated when analysis and reporting tools are successfully applied. This not only enables managers to view which specific factors are driving margin or cost, but also allows them to make a direct connection to the report card published quarterly to shareholders.

PRINCIPLE IN ACTION

For Bill Braddy, Vice President of Engineering and Knowledge Services for Schneider Logistics, having the right facts at the right time and presented within clearly understood parameters can make all the difference between keeping and losing a customer.

He explains: "If we can make our information system present the same facts to all parties simultaneously, then we can collectively act, collaborate, and make decisions based on this common view of the facts."

But, for Braddy, it goes beyond simply sharing the facts. It means getting the right facts at the right time to make the most informed decision. "Otherwise," says Braddy, "if a decision is made too late, the outcome is wasted. However, if the decision is made based on immature data, the decision could quite likely be wrong. For instance, if a decision to abandon a customer relationship because of failed performance comes too late in the decision cycle, then the value of that decision is lost. In reality, this decision should happen at a time when service and costs are only beginning to become imbalanced,

when we can still try to find ways to change the outcomes so we don't have to part ways."

By connecting once disparate data sources—for example, labor tracking, purchasing, and warranty—and empowering users to interact with the data themselves, Schneider employees can conduct studies across different data sources to ensure they have the most appropriate information at the right time to make an informed decision. They can access information in a time frame that has value, with many studies that took weeks—even months—now becoming routine across the business.

Respect Instinct, Experience, and Talent

Most decisions are typically informed by a decision-maker's own instinct. But when it comes to managing a high-performance business, instinct and experience must be applied to fact. And the facts must come first.

Business decision-making has always relied on a formula that takes into account the savvy and experience of the decision-maker, a formula where decisions are often made by the seat of the pants. While

> **Having the right facts at the right time and presented within clearly understood parameters can make all the difference between keeping and losing a customer.**

this style of decision-making may seem outmoded, it remains the primary means by which decisions are made in business today. In an independent survey commissioned expressly for this book, we found that the majority of business people inform decisions with instinct, input from colleagues, and input from direct reports.

The problem with these methods is twofold. First, decision-makers today are unlikely to own all of the information that informs their decisions. With the increasing link-up of companies and systems across the value chain, it is becoming impossible for decision-makers to be aware of all the forces impacting a decision and all the ways in which their decision impacts the business.

The days of driving business primarily by instinct were the days when decision-makers could meet their customers face-to-face and walk the shop floor without having to travel halfway around the world to do it. However, as decision-makers become increasingly distanced from customers and the means of production, they become more dependent on hard facts to make a decision. You cannot put your hand on an Internet cable and take the pulse of your business—and today you need to take many pulses at once.

The second problem is that if instinct outweighs fact in decision-making, decision-makers may not be getting the maximum value from the masses of information—the data—that make up the company at its most fundamental level. In such a scenario, managers are not only making business decisions that are largely uninformed, but also failing to leverage the rich wellspring of resources that are at their fingertips.

So how does a company feed instinct into its information infrastructure? Instinct and experience are based upon facts—typically the facts as you've experienced them on some other conscious level or at some other point in time. Consequently, it is possible to break instinct and experience down into logical chunks of data that can be used by others. When one asks the question, "Why does my instinct tell me to do X when the data says Y?" the answer is rarely a mystery. It's simply that you are applying the data of your own discrete experiences to a situation—and doing so from a purely subconscious level. Once this question has been answered, new data, information, business rules, or changes to existing business rules can suddenly be factored into other decision points. In this way, experience and instinct are actually instantiated into your information infrastructure. This undertaking can be supported and tested using technology such as modeling software to see whether the instinct has been well defined and whether acting contrary to instinct would have brought about the same result.

> **With the increasing link-up of companies and systems across the value chain, it is becoming impossible for decision-makers to be aware of all the forces impacting a decision and all the ways in which their decision impacts the business.**

PRINCIPLE 6 | **BALANCE FINANCIAL AND NON-FINANCIAL DRIVERS**

From sponsorship to crew safety, high-performance yacht racing demands a balanced view of every essential performance driver—even those that don't directly impact the vessel's bottom line: speed.

Running a high-performance business requires a balanced view of every essential business driver—even those that don't directly impact the bottom line.

By the time a problem shows up on the balance sheet, it may be too late to stop it. Running a high-performance business requires a balanced view of every essential business driver—even those that don't directly impact the bottom line. Unfortunately, companies often set up key groups of decision-makers to work at cross-purposes because of the data they use and the manner in which they are organized.

Senior management teams almost always focus on what impacts the bottom line. By contrast, other decision-makers—like line-of-business managers, analysts, and knowledge workers— are focused primarily on non-financial, more qualitative performance concerns, such as the tasks they must accomplish or the problems they must fix. For instance, these individuals must cope with more operational issues such as, "How many times this month did our production line stall, and is that new equipment we just bought helping at all?" and "How are we doing with our customers… are they defecting to that hot new competitor? If not, why are they staying?"

Non-financial information about business performance acts as an early-warning (or early-opportunity) system for the financial information that ultimately expresses the performance of the business. And while non-financial information has a direct impact on financial results, it is far more difficult to measure. Evolving trends and shifts in the way the company is being managed tend to

arise not at the level of financial reports, but as subtle shifts in customer profitability, in certain distribution channels, or in particular divisions. Largely unobserved, this information represents missed opportunities to exploit cash-rich business or remedy performance-hampering problems. Responding to these shifts means recognizing the value of non-financial, qualitative information and then having systems in place to track them, so you can

> **High-performance companies educate themselves in the art of dynamic adjustment by constantly tracking the pulse of performance at key points throughout the company.**

adjust dynamically to change as and when it happens. High-performance companies educate themselves in the art of dynamic adjustment by constantly tracking the pulse of performance at key points throughout the company.

In the same way that collaboration and integration are key ingredients for a high-performance enterprise, so too are financial and non-financial performance indicators indispensable and interdependent. To integrate the two, a business's key functions and processes must be tied back to company performance. It is a performance imperative that must be hardwired into the decision-making practices of every manager.

LAYING THE FOUNDATION

Develop Your Levers and Drivers

There are a number of formalized methodologies for evaluating business performance at the senior management level: Kaplan and Norton's balanced scorecard and the Six Sigma program popularized by General Electric are two well-known examples. And while each is distinct from the other in its approach—and from other less formal approaches—they have one key thing in common: the requirement to understand and declare the critical performance drivers of an organization and the combinations of factors that have the greatest impact upon them.

For the high-performance business, "job one" is to:

1. Identify the key processes and functions of the company. Look for the cross-functional touch points and how they impact the process.
2. Identify the high-value drivers of the business. This is trickier than it sounds as many companies risk selecting lower value drivers or drivers that support management's gut feel of the business. This is the time for some corporate soul-searching.
3. Set clear, measurable targets for these drivers that can be monitored and reported upon on a regular basis. Ensure that managers with accountability over impacting these drivers are also accountable for working toward the targets that have been established.

PRINCIPLE IN ACTION

Harrah's uses an elaborate customer satisfaction measurement system that focuses on the customers most profitable to the company—thereby creating a direct correlation between less tangible factors such as customer satisfaction and the company's bottom line. Simply put, the happier the client, the more money that person is likely to spend at one of Harrah's operations.

Gary Loveman, Chief Operating Officer, explains that "while it's not a random sample in the true sense of the word, it's a random sample of customers we care the most about. It's administered in a variety of ways, and the data is collected and analyzed weekly and shared with the units of each business weekly. So, for example, the valet parkers in St. Louis have a weekly measure of how they are being rated on their friendliness and their speed of service: two critical attributes of our business."

> **Harrah's uses an elaborate customer satisfaction measurement system that focuses on the company's most profitable customers—thereby creating a direct correlation between less tangible factors such as customer satisfaction and the company's bottom line.**

HIGH-PERFORMANCE MANAGEMENT

Management is the intersection where people and practices meet. When both are fine-tuned for effective collaboration and integration, your business will benefit from high-performance management. This final section brings together the principles we've looked at so far to create a vision for holistic, effective performance management across the extended enterprise.

PRINCIPLE 7 | FOSTER PERFORMANCE NETWORKS

High-performance yacht racing demands that every individual and every function be interconnected to ensure seamless execution and instantaneous response to changing conditions.

A chain is only as strong as its weakest link. A network, however, is as strong as its richest resource.

A large U.K.-based chain of supermarkets recently discovered a critical performance-driving relationship between beer and baby products. Using state-of-the-art query and analysis tools, the organization discovered that the sales timing of the two products is unexpectedly synchronized. The findings are not a fluke. It turns out that when daddy goes to the supermarket to buy "nappies," he also takes the opportunity to grab a few beers for himself.

This cultural reality would have been completely invisible to the supermarket chain had it not been able to correlate and analyze seemingly disparate data from different suppliers. Because it was able to do so, it reorganized its supermarkets to capitalize on the trend—and doubled its sales of both products as a result.

In the past, the business performance management role was typically associated with more senior tiers of management. Today, people at all levels of a company's organization chart must make and share decisions that impact the value chain, for it is they who reside at the point of impact—at the information sweet spot. For all intents and purposes, these people are "managers"—no matter what their job title—because they are also decision-makers who are linked to a virtual team that contributes to specific key performance indicators.

On a typical corporate organization chart, people have clear linear attachment to those above and below them; only occasionally are lateral lines drawn between individuals across different departments. The org chart tends to be geared toward controlling the flow of information and decision-making, rather than enriching business performance. When decision-makers are hierarchically fused in departmental silos, with little control over the lateral impact they have, bottlenecks, information hoarding, and other "weak links" eventually undermine the entire decision chain.

What companies are beginning to understand is that the lateral lines are just as important to performance as the vertical ones. This is particularly true in instances where key functional areas like HR, manufacturing, inventory,

Today, people at all levels of a company's organization chart must make and share decisions that impact the value chain, for it is they who reside at the point of impact.

and logistics are farmed out to specialist companies. These networks of cross-functional decision-makers—or performance networks—almost always impact some aspect of company performance. For instance, a VP of marketing would know to consult with the VP of R&D before a new product is publicly launched.

Typically, however, it is a group of people rather than individuals who contribute to a particular area of business performance—i.e., they contribute to common key performance indicators (KPIs). Each individual within such a group—or "performance unit"—owns specific levers such as customers, geographical areas, or product responsibility, each of which directly impacts performance measures owned by other people in the unit. In other words, these "performance units" own a shared management perspective on the business—with shared goals and a shared approach to decision-making, empowerment, and execution.

Performance networks are vastly augmented when decision-makers are physically linked in a network of shared information. This not only enables accelerated validation and execution, but ultimately helps companies bypass decision roadblocks associated with more outmoded approaches to decision-making, such as decision-by-committee.

LAYING THE FOUNDATION

Network Your Decision-Makers

Most decisions, regardless of their simplicity or complexity, rarely happen in a vacuum. In reality, they tend to intersect with one another to create a fluid and constantly expanding web. Decisions and decision-makers are not simply interconnected—they are also interdependent.

The notion that decision-makers are fundamentally interconnected is nothing new. However, as new business realities demand increasing reliance on integration and collaboration, this interconnectedness only becomes more important. The emergence of intranets and extranets, and networking in general, has only further entrenched the importance of interconnectedness into the corporate mindset while expanding this connectivity out to partners, suppliers, even customers.

A network is essentially a community-driven entity comprising people and processes that share a common purpose and follow common rules—much like a highway system whose purpose is the safe transportation of people and product. Highway systems are built around common rules that must be consistently applied and followed. In North America, drivers on a two-way highway must stick to the right side of the road at all times. In the U.K., the rules require that drivers stay to the left. In both instances, the actual rule isn't as important as the fact that everyone drives consistently.

Similarly, information networks have become critical to business performance because they enable a shared context for everyone across the value chain. An enterprise that doesn't operate with a shared purpose and shared business rules can find itself

> **The emergence of intranets and extranets, and networking in general, has only further entrenched the importance of interconnectedness into the corporate mindset while expanding this connectivity out to partners, suppliers, even customers.**

and its partners driving down the wrong side of the highway—or driving down the wrong highway altogether.

A performance network is a network approach to management and decision-making that adopts networks as the technical backbone through which decisions and information are conveyed between decision-makers. The purpose of the link-up is to embed performance management into the decisions made across the extended business on a minute-by-minute basis.

On top of this foundation sits a dimensional framework, a data structure organized to represent the performance hierarchies of the company. It is fed by various data sources and unites cross-functional categories such as customer, product, and territory into a consistent, enterprise-wide view. This layer, in turn, feeds analysis based on a common terminology—whether you are in the sales, finance, or inventory department—and on clearly understood parameters for success.

Networking decision-makers in this way supports an enterprise model for performance-driven decision-making. In this scenario, users are provided with their own unique blend of information while, at the same time, consistent information is shared across the enterprise. The result is effective, coordinated, and collaborative decision-making.

Consistent Data and Shared Context

Consistent data is a fundamental requirement for effective, collaborative decision-making. But only when data is placed within a framework, or context, does it ultimately provide true value as information. If a friend approaches you and says "keys! table!" they're not relaying information in the most useful way. If, however, your friend places the concepts of "keys" and "table" within a context by saying "your car keys are on the table," suddenly he or she is conveying information that could be of considerably greater value.

Applying context to data essentially means packaging raw data into manageable bundles, then applying the appropriate business terminology and structures so that it becomes consumable and consistent.

A good illustration of this would be to ask someone to try to understand the implications of all the information contained in the corporate databases, transaction systems, spreadsheets, and data warehouses—simply by looking at data rows. It would be a protracted, painful, and ultimately futile effort. Unless data is contextualized, and thereby given meaning, it is virtually useless to us. It is for this reason that context is as critical as data itself. Together, they create information that has purpose and is actionable.

Information = Data + Context

Context becomes especially important when you extend your performance network out to other companies, particularly those that use transactional systems that not only are incompatible with yours, but also are beyond your control. How do you guarantee the quality of the decisions that are made along the value chain? You do it by sharing context and consistent data across a decision network.

Information networks have become critical to business performance as they enable a shared context for everyone across the value chain.

Let's explore another example. If you were to read a report that referenced the past "year," could you tell immediately if the term referred to the fiscal year or the calendar year? What if the report had no title? In other words, does the meaning of the word differ depending on what report it appears in? And what is the relationship between the data under these two measures of time—fiscal and calendar?

Defining context means creating a frame of reference. This requires defining each term in its own right and then determining how each term interrelates. By doing so, you would—upon hearing the category "year"—immediately understand its reference. Ambiguity would be eliminated, for you, for other managers, and for your suppliers, partners, or customers. When it comes to defining complex terms like "profitability," this knowledge becomes particularly valuable.

Looking at "units sold" from the vantage point of customers, you can find out who is buying what. Looking at it from the point of view of time, you can get an idea of the sales cycle. Combining these dimensions by intersecting time, customer, and location with a particular product will tell you a lot more about sales of the product. For example, do particular clients buy in a specific time frame in a specific location? By combining dimensions, you create a common context by which you can understand the information that feeds your business—a common context for decision-making.

The value of performance networks lies in their ability to support high-performance management by interconnecting decision-makers, regardless of how a business is structured. A performance network can span everything from a small team of five people to entire marketplaces. It enables consistent, coordinated decision-making across any collective of decision-makers, even if they are geographically dispersed or working for separate companies.

Performance networks help you make effective decisions—decisions that can help accelerate the growth of your company. But, just as importantly, they help you make effective decisions by giving you easy access to the information you need.

How do you guarantee the quality of the decisions that are made along the value chain? You do it by sharing context and consistent data across a decision network.

This can take the form of alerts that notify you of exceptional information, problems, and opportunities. It can also take the form of analytics that provide the tools you need to easily explore, analyze, and understand information.

Effective decision-making also means being able to instantly share insights, conclusions, and the full value of the decision across the department, company, or value chain. Finally, it means knowing that every decision you make is valid and, what's more, can be instantly validated by any other decision-maker in your decision network. When these capabilities are in place, you can conduct business intelligently and with precision.

Moreover, by recognizing and fostering these networks of decision-makers, you can bolster performance and optimize business processes without having to change your corporate structure. It is a high-value undertaking that has minimal physical impact on the organization of your company.

PRINCIPLE IN ACTION

NCR's recent move to company-wide information management is a compelling example of performance networks at work. Based on the development of a central data warehouse, NCR has built an information infrastructure that provides integrated global information to decision-makers across the entire value chain. The purpose of this move was to reinforce consistent worldwide operating processes and drive process improvements. NCR recognized early on that this undertaking would require the ability to deliver standard performance measures and contextualized information across the business.

As discussed under our second principle, NCR's "mean time to repair" performance indicator—critical for NCR's customers—was not consistently tracked or defined around the world. This made it extremely difficult to understand what was causing a delay or another customer service problem. Today, nearly every NCR customer services operation around the world looks at this measure the same way at every level of management. They

can also quickly drill down to the information relevant to their role in the performance network—like individual product, customer, or service call.

By combining an innovative technology infrastructure with its evolving business model and decision culture, NCR is empowering groups of decision-makers to collaborate using consistent, contextualized information. Customer services managers generate detailed customer-focused profit and loss statements from financial and other operational sources, then analyze revenue details, part costs, and labor. Services sales and account support managers collaborate to manage customer growth and profitability using a consistent, understandable process.

> **By combining an innovative technology infrastructure with its evolving business model and decision culture, NCR is empowering groups of decision-makers to collaborate using consistent, contextualized information.**

NCR's engineering organization is also recognized as a key member of its customer service performance network. As such, key customer services metrics related to product quality are shared with engineering to help drive design improvements.

By enacting the principles of the high-performance business, NCR is realizing its strategic shift to becoming a high-performance enterprise.

PRINCIPLE 8 | DESIGN YOUR DECISION CULTURE

High-performance yachts are designed to maximize speed, agility, and responsiveness. Crews are trained and equipped to ensure that everyone—captain, helmsman, navigator, grinders, and others—has insight, and input, into their shared world.

Create a culture around decision-making where everyone—managers, knowledge workers, executives, partners, suppliers, and customers—has insight into their shared world.

Companies that are aware of their current decision culture can deliberately create a culture around decision-making where everyone—managers, knowledge workers, executives, partners, suppliers, and customers—has insight into their shared world. The result of such a culture is high-performance decision-making, for a high-performance business.

What Is Decision Culture?

Decision culture refers to the particular style of management and decision-making that is used by a team, department, business unit, company, public-sector organization, or supply-chain relationship. Every company has one—your company has one. The trick is to recognize it and decide if it is the healthiest culture for your company.

A decision culture is characterized by the traits or behaviors exhibited by decision-makers within any given business structure. Like other types of business culture, the behavior and expectations of management are the greatest contributors to its definition and design. In particular, a decision culture is defined by:

- The degree to which information is shared
- How it is shared
- The breadth of information that is used to inform decisions
- How decisions are validated and enacted

Think Forum Before Form

As indicated in Principle 2, managers are naturally inclined to try to put their hands around the entire business, to get things under control, to get "back to basics." When this happens, companies tend to reorganize, reengineer, and restructure in an attempt to regain a sense of control.

But if what you are really looking to do is collaborate, how you structure your organization is less important than ensuring your people have a mechanism in place to talk to each other, as well as to partners, suppliers, and customers. Likewise, if you need to integrate, it makes no sense to build new teams of people who aren't willing or able to share insight and knowledge. If you seek to innovate, to become a high-performance business, you need a cultural setting and an information infrastructure that supports creativity, flexibility—even zealotry. This can happen only when you focus on creating a collaborative forum for decision-makers, rather than on locking down the form or structure of your organization.

> **Every company has a decision culture—your company has one. The trick is to recognize it and decide if it's the healthiest culture for your company.**

Everyone Has a Decision Culture

Almost every company has at least one of the following decision cultures lurking somewhere in the organization. None are particularly unusual, and together they provide a frame for understanding the concept of decision culture, by seeing how it plays itself out in your organization.

1 | Committee Culture

If the most commonly heard phrase in your office is "let's meet about that," and you find yourself in recurrent meetings whose outcomes are never certain, you are probably experiencing committee culture.

The committee culture is characterized by meetings intended to determine what everyone else knows. Today, this task is better left to a technology-based forum such as a corporate portal, a database, and business intelligence systems.

The upside to this decision culture is that everyone typically takes comfort in the fact that all bases have been covered and, more importantly, that they have been included in the decision-making process. It is a highly collaborative culture, in which everyone (or, at least, everyone in a particular meeting) possesses the same information as everyone else.

The downside is twofold: First, the information that everyone shares may be wrong. Although people in such a culture have a sense of assurance that all bases are covered, this is not necessarily true—particularly since personality can strongly influence this type of decision culture. For instance, one person may tend to dominate the committee, in which case he or she is really dictating the content of the group's knowledge.

Secondly, if no course of action or decision emerges despite ongoing information sharing, the efficacy of the entire practice should probably be questioned. The result of this type of culture is often slow, unbalanced decision-making that lacks appropriate context or objective data. The absence of goals in these meetings also tends to reflect a lack of strong leadership and vision, which is essential for taking the decision—and the company—forward.

2 | Instinct Culture

History is full of examples of ill-conceived decisions and erroneous predictions that were based mostly on the experience or instinct of a decision-maker. Some of these predictions have achieved cult status. Now infamous, for instance, is the underestimation that IBM's Thomas Watson made regarding computing ubiquity: "I think there is a world market for maybe five computers." Also infamous is the statement made by Ken Olson, president and founder of Digital Equipment Corporation: "There is no reason anyone would want a computer in their home."

An instinct-driven decision culture is characterized by highly qualitative, but often unbalanced, decision-making. Success in this environment depends upon an individual decision-maker's intuition in their area of accountability, which is largely the product of experience. Thus, by definition, decision-making power cannot be passed on to new managers and subordinates,

> **In an instinct-driven decision culture, where decision-making tends to be enacted in a seat-of-the-pants fashion, the entire structure is only as strong as its weakest link.**

thereby inhibiting the distribution of decision-making power.

In an instinct-driven decision culture, where decision-making tends to be enacted in a seat-of-the-pants fashion, the entire structure is only as strong as its weakest link. If the person calling the shots on a particular decision is relying on instinct alone and his or her gut feeling is wrong, every subsequent decision down the command structure becomes founded on a faulty premise. Considerable time and resources could be wasted before this faulty premise is identified. More importantly, critical opportunities may be missed.

It is necessary to note here that, in a decision culture supported by a performance network, this equation is turned on its head. Because of its very nature as a network, the entire structure is as strong as its most experienced decision-maker. The experience of senior decision-makers is built into the entire context of the network in its development phase and continually strengthened via the feedback loop. At the same time, the network enables decisions to be validated quickly, using data as the key proof point, while ensuring collaboration around the decision by bringing to bear the experience of many on a single, focused decision.

3 | Bottleneck Culture

The primary characteristics of the bottleneck decision culture are the slow pace with which decisions are made and the lack of trust that prevents distributed ownership of business performance and, therefore, of the business model. In this type of environment, certain stakeholders often wield decision-making power merely as a result of an assumption that they be included, not because they actually own any particular decision point. Contrary to today's business trend, decision-making in this environment tends to be deferred up in the organization, rather than down and across. Nothing can be validated without this person's or that person's approval.

The fundamental issue in this situation is trust—one individual is perceived to hold the golden decision-making egg, and nobody else can act without this person's input. This situation may, on the surface, resemble collaboration or teamwork—"Let's make sure that our counterparts in departments X and Y are happy with this too." It is, in fact, just the opposite. Rather than working together to reach a meaningful conclusion, this decision culture tends to pit one person or one group's opinion against another group's, hoping for an outcome that is not too watered down.

In this situation, we see a perfect example of the violation of our third principle: empower at the point of impact. The decision role of the individual decision-maker does not intersect appropriately with the level of decisions they are making. The result of this scenario is familiar to many of us: willingly or not, one or two individuals become roadblocks to getting on with business. This can pose a serious threat to business performance.

Of course, nobody continues to do something ineffective unless they are getting some kind of payback from it. The upside of a bottleneck decision culture is that the management team has a handle on the progress of the organization, and thus has much tighter perceived control than in a situation where decision-making is more autonomous and distributed.

The downside is that, in spite of a well-buffered comfort and control zone, change and action take much longer to initiate in this kind of environment. Innovation may be paid lip service but is almost impossible to achieve. For example, lower level managers and knowledge workers with good ideas often cannot get an audience with the people who should be hearing them, let alone help the company create new sources of value.

4 | Knowledge-Hoarding Culture

Mary arrives at a meeting armed with facts, charts, and, of course, the open eyes and ears of management. She has a great system for obtaining and interpreting data and she uses it to her advantage: either to advance her career or to justify larger investments in her area, which—to her credit—is one of the most productive in the organization. She's considered sharing her approach with her counterparts in other departments, but her slice of the pie would be significantly smaller if she did. It is a question of priorities, and a matter of politics—the politics of withholding information for power and manipulation.

"Information Is Power"

It isn't that information is no longer a source of power. But the means by which information provides power are changing. In business, information held is often power lost. For example, how long would companies like IBM, American Express, and RJR Nabisco be successful if they kept information out of the hands of their partners, distributors, and customers? How quickly would popular Web browsers such as Microsoft's Internet Explorer and Netscape's Navigator have been adopted if they hadn't been offered free? Would we have recognized the true impact of the Internet—as both a communications and a business-enabling tool—if it wasn't assumed that people already had access?

Hoarding information may seem advantageous. But what happens if others are better positioned to positively impact the business based on your knowledge? A shared asset can provide everyone with the chance to drive success.

In the era of Internet-enabled information access, information shared is power galvanized. This is particularly true for organizations seeking to share key performance data with their business partners. By allowing partners to see how your distribution channel is performing, what your current inventory stock levels are or the latest customer satisfaction survey on your touchstone product, you create a new kind of business relationship between you and your partners—a relationship that has the best interests of both in mind.

> **In the era of Internet-enabled information access, information shared is power galvanized. This is particularly true for organizations seeking to share key performance data with their business partners.**

In a knowledge-hoarding culture, information and knowledge are very closely aligned with authority. People do not share what they know, they invest it. They invest it in entitlement and privilege, in promises of future preference, pay increases, or other types of exclusive returns. In this culture, information is the property of an individual or an exclusive group of individuals, and everyone wants to hold on to such assets as long as they can.

As with all decision cultures, there's an upside to the knowledge-hoarding culture. For one, function-focused decisions are highly informed and consistent within the individual function—this is certainly the case with Mary—as it is in the hoarder's best interest to invest his or her knowledge in the success of the group to which they're attached.

Often, however, a knowledge-hoarding decision culture is symptomatic of a corporate culture built around internal competition. This self-consuming competition may be specific to a single business unit or generalized throughout the company as a whole. The product development team is fed up with the senior management team's basing its decisions on what the marketing department is saying. The customer service staff questions some of the half-baked promises marketing has made in its latest television ad. Sales can't believe the kind of inventory delays it has to deal with—it's losing clients by the minute. Regional offices are fed up with everyone, so they decide to just do their own thing.

A knowledge-hoarding decision culture is one in which the silos that result from a poorly designed corporate culture inevitably lead to uncoordinated decision-making. High-performance management is virtually impossible, particularly when it comes to tracking real performance—for the simple reason that nobody is talking. Reporting is centered on the success of individuals and individual functions, not on the business as a whole.

LAYING THE FOUNDATION

Foster Decision Culture Awareness

Companies often design particular corporate cultures. This can be a very conscious and explicit undertaking. Alternatively, it can be a backdrop or a strategic principle that guides "the way we do things around here." A decision culture, on the other hand, is relatively invisible—primarily because it is not typically regarded as separate from corporate culture. Few businesses are explicitly conscious of what their decision culture looks like. Fewer have even considered the nature of their decision culture.

> **The moment you realize that a decision culture exists or that you can be explicit about the decision culture you want to have, you can effect significant change in your organization.**

Being aware of your decision culture and what it is or isn't doing for your company is critically important. "Being aware" means two things:

- Understanding that you have a decision culture or cultures

- Being deliberate about designing an effective decision culture

In both instances, the key is to have a conscious understanding of how your decision culture impacts your business. The moment you realize that a decision culture exists or that you can be explicit about the decision culture you want to have, you can effect significant change in your organization.

Think for a moment about how decisions are made in your company. Chances are, there are a few elements you would like to change. But to apply change, you must first understand your current decision culture. And to understand your decision culture, it becomes essential to recognize how decisions are made in your company by discerning what drives decision-making, the relationship of information to decision-making, and the perspective from which this information is regarded. It means asking yourself some basic yet critical questions:

- What role does leadership play in designing a culture of innovation?
- How are decisions made in your company?
- How is information shared?
- To what extent is information coordinated?
- What are your parameters for success? Do you have explicit parameters?
- Do you use common metrics to measure success?
- Do you use a common language to describe success?
- How are decisions validated and rationalized?

PRINCIPLE IN ACTION

"If you want a powerful decision-making model, all approaches pale in comparison to the need for an organization to put in place a mechanism, catalyst, willingness, strategy for embracing change," says Bill Braddy, Vice President of Engineering and Knowledge Services, Schneider Logistics, Inc.

Almost any senior executive knows that resistance to change is the biggest block to corporate innovation. "If it means change, it must be bad," or "that's not the way I've always done it," or the classic, "don't fix what isn't broken." The problem, however, is that it is difficult to identify what's broken unless you change your perspective of the business.

As Braddy points out: "If you make no change to today's behavior, tomorrow's performance is pretty predictable—it will be the same as today's. If you want different results, you have to look at things differently."

Greasing the wheels of resistance must happen in such a way that it benefits the company without alienating employees. There are two approaches to doing this: deploy powerful leadership and validate strategy with results. Both counteract resistance to change by aiming right at the heart of the problem: showing people what's in it for them. In this way, it is possible to begin steering the company's decision culture in a new direction.

The key to changing behaviors is to set conditions for change. It seems simple in theory, but as Braddy has learned, it is not so straightforward in reality:

"Generally one of two things will happen: the conditions for change will come from the top down and if you can't find yourself willing to meet the conditions, you should find yourself another company. In other words, a dynamic, Jack Welch -type leader can come in and remove the alternatives, the 'things the way we've always done them.' But, in the absence of a Jack Welch, the data must be made so overwhelming that the decision to make the change is no longer a decision, but a default. Obsolescence can be the mother of fundamental corporate change."

Schneider Logistics combined both of these approaches by enabling its people to see the value of consistent, collaborative business performance management. It did this by first appealing to the primary pain point of each employee: the absence of consistent information to inform decision-making. Initially, senior management made a decision to change the way warranties were tracked and recovered. By creating an information analysis infrastructure around its warranty system, Schneider was able to achieve 100% return on investment in under a year. In this undertaking, it linked up its repair parts system, internal labor-tracking system, and purchasing department with its warranty claim and reimbursement system. All of a sudden, analysts were able to see the percentage of their costs that were recovered from vendors, as well as labor and parts recovery by vendor, part, operating center, product model, and much more—in a matter of hours as opposed to days or months. Over the two years that the system has been in place, Schneider has tracked and audited a savings of $2 to $3 million in unnecessary costs.

When Schneider showed these results—and reimbursement checks—to its people, most of the resistance to change melted away. Suddenly, people realized that their lives would be easier, that the savings they achieved actually benefited the company in a measurable way. The decision culture began to shift because people came to see themselves as contributors to the company's overall performance rather than workers responsible for a list of tasks. "After that," explains Braddy, "the change acceptance process becomes more evolutionary than revolutionary. Coupled with relentless pressure for innovation, vision, and strategy, this approach showed our people what they could get out of dramatic change."

> **The key to changing behaviors is to set conditions for change. It seems simple in theory, but as Braddy has learned, it is not so straightforward in reality.**

Another example is Harrah's Entertainment, Inc., which has deployed a unique approach to designing its decision culture. Like Schneider's, Harrah's approach is successful because it demonstrates the value of changing "the way things are done" in a way that is clear and relevant to decision-makers at all levels of the organization—including people on the frontlines of customer service.

Valet parkers, for instance, receive a weekly measure of how they are being rated on their friendliness and speed of service. This program is called the "Performance Payout." All of the properties are financially incented to support this program, which has paid out in excess of $10 million in bonuses to frontline employees across the company over the last two years. When employees improve the level of measured satisfaction Harrah's guests receive, they score points that translate into paid bonuses.

This kind of program is profitable only in a company that can track customer service information at the speed of its business. The transformation was driven by Harrah's commitment to becoming a company founded on impeccable management of its customer relationships. By deploying systems and approaches that enable decision-makers across the company to understand this performance and how their activities impact it, Harrah's has also transformed its decision culture.

"Our decision culture is completely different today. In fact, it has been a cathartic effort," explains Harrah's COO, Gary Loveman. "The people who run these businesses were raised around facilities. When I started, you visited a general manager and the first thing he'd want to do was take you on a tour. He'd show you how the hot dog stand that was over here has been moved to the right, and explain how he's sure that will make a big difference. He'd explain how the fountain that went straight up now goes sideways. It was all about facilities. Today, we still take the tour occasionally—but we talk about what's happening with

customers. We talk about what our behavioral data tell us about the decisions customers are making. The reporting systems we have give us longitudinal behavior data on our customers. So we know which customers have changed their behavior, and why. When I see revenues were supposed to be up 5% in Chicago and they're up only 3%, we're going to sit down and say, 'OK, why did that happen?' And we can really identify the answer, with great accuracy, because our systems are linked up and our people are speaking one language. This lets us focus on how we fix problems, which is now what my managers worry about, by and large. That's their role, and specialists now take on the facilities piece of it. As a result, our facilities have also gotten noticeably better."

> **By deploying systems and approaches that enable decision-makers across the company to understand this performance and how their activities impact it, Harrah's has also transformed its decision culture.**

By combining a strong strategy with availability of information, Harrah's transformed itself. It created a truth contract that dictated how it was going to make money, how it was going to grow. It decided that it would grow by changing the decisions consumers make, which meant changing the way Harrah's made decisions. Its decision culture is now centered on the strongest performance driver in its business—customer relationship management.

CONCLUSION

Harrah's, Hunter Douglas, NCR, and Schneider Logistics are only a few of the world's innovative, performance-driven companies building their management and decision-making approaches around the principles discussed in this book.

They understand and have embraced the fundamentals of these principles, recognizing that to shape a coherent strategy for profitable growth means engaging every corner of the enterprise. It demands tight integration of systems, processes, and people so as to breed innovation and identify new sources of value no matter where they may reside. It requires meaningful collaboration across functions, regions, even companies, so as to exploit every opportunity and overcome every challenge—with speed and with confidence.

This is no easy task, as each of these companies has discovered. Increased competition and market volatility are pushing organizations around the globe to discard traditional business models in favor of new and sometimes untested assumptions. Today, companies are finding that success is not measured by financial statements alone, but also by less quantifiable metrics such as customer satisfaction. They realize that they must uncover new methods of communication that drive the right information to the right people, whether employees, partners, or customers. And that they must build an infrastructure to make this information relevant and meaningful to all.

And yet a high-performance company is not built by technology alone. It must come from within. Employees need to embrace change. To be able to do that, they need a clear understanding of how their decisions contribute to the overall performance of the business. High-performance companies strive to build a culture based on trust, where decisions gravitate to the point of impact instead of up the chain of command.

Executives must articulate their vision across the enterprise and support their employees in achieving that vision with the right tools and training and the autonomy to act. The challenges they face are many: delayed action due to a centralized, top-down, or tentative decision culture; confusion born of unclear parameters for performance measurement; isolation arising from the inability to speak a common language internally and externally; and—overshadowing all—the accelerating pace of business.

But when the payoff is winning the race, it is worth the investment. Around the globe, high-performance organizations are finding out, every day, why it pays to invest in creating a collaborative and integrated performance network. The principles discussed in this book are offered as a starting point: a framework for forging new relationships between people and a clear understanding of the underlying forces that impel a business toward success or failure. They introduce a marriage of ideas and infrastructure that—together—form the basis of the high-performance enterprise.

Imagine…Going from Discovery to Action in Five Days

Marina Sanchez, a senior product manager at Crescent Integration International (CII), gazed at her computer screen. She was still amazed by the wealth of information available through her Enterprise Information Portal (EIP). A year or so of concentrated work and exceptional cooperation between the information technology group and business users at CII had culminated in the launch of the company's information portal. Finally, decision-makers across the company could access critical information about the business, develop a common understanding of the factors that impacted performance, and make decisions quickly and effectively.

CII is in the business of providing assembly and integration services to a global client base within the telecommunications and computer industries. These services include printed circuit assembly, full-system assembly, packaging, and distribution services. Marina, a veteran of the industry, had been a senior product manager with CII for the past five years, managing a portfolio of similar products "from cradle to grave." She was also a member of the Information Systems steering committee that had spent the last year developing its Decision Modeling System (DMS), which packaged the company's key information for its decision-makers.

Through the company's portal, the Decision Modeling System pushed information about revenues, sales, new client development, and the revenue contribution of new products to the desktops of managers. It also provided external information like stock market reports and industry-specific financial benchmarks.

CII managers could also pull specific information from a variety of databases and other information sources, such as sales, finance, and production data marts. From these internal data marts, they could review key performance indicators like inventory on hand, on-time shipments, sales force distribution, and advertising/marketing expenditures. They could review in-depth industry and customer marketing information from external sources such as Dun & Bradstreet and Standard & Poor's, as well as explore selected data marts from some of their strategic partners. And they could share the results of their analyses with others inside CII and across the value chain.

Based on the information Marina had just received from the EIP about her product portfolio, CII's Decision Modeling System would once again have to earn its keep. Marina would soon need to make a number of key product decisions.

The Company

CII is a market leader in electronics manufacturing services, with a global client base in the telecommunications and computer industries. The company's services include printed circuit assembly, full systems assembly, packaging, and distribution services. Its core business is the assembly of components for original equipment manufacturers (OEMs). CII has captured a large share of the market by demonstrating a strong ability to creatively manage production, staffing, and product delivery to suit clients' quality and performance needs.

The company's business model is to contract out functions and processes it doesn't consider a core business competency. For example, some aspects of human resources management are contracted out, as are some production functions. However, CII maintains its in-house information services and IT functions, believing that information management is a critical asset in the company's ability to compete and win. This strategy has turned CII into an extremely flexible organization supported by a strong information-processing backbone that helps to coordinate activities across the various operating units.

CII has assembly plants in New Hampshire, Boston, Mexico, Thailand, Brazil, the U.K., and China. Revenues in the last fiscal year were in the order of $3 billion, and the company hopes to double its size to $6 billion within the next three years, requiring year-over-year revenue growth of 27%.

DAY 1: DISCOVERY AND ANALYSIS

The alert Marina had just received showed that one of the key products in CII's portfolio appeared to be reaching maturity. She was faced with making a decision about a potential new source of revenue to replace this flagship product. To do this, she would need to track the product life cycle in the company's client product portfolio.

Prior to the portal's availability, Marina would have faced the daunting task of having to both compile and translate raw data drawn from several disconnected sources—internally across CII's various departments and externally across CII's many suppliers and distributors. This would have required considerable time and resources, not only to gather the information, but to then make sense of it.

Establishing the appropriate linkages—first between departments within the company and then with its suppliers, distributors, and clients—had taken considerable time and a lot of negotiation, but it had been well worth the effort. Now Marina could see almost immediately when certain products were reaching maturity and would need investment or repositioning in order to prolong their life cycles.

The portal armed her with the facts she needed to identify potential issues before they impacted the company's performance. It also let her quickly access sufficient data to pinpoint alternative revenue-generating opportunities and to determine the key parameters required to translate that opportunity into action.

The latest sales report showed that sales of the once-popular ToughBoard had peaked. This component was designed for use in products like notebook computers, which had to stand up to the bumps, scrapes, and general abuse inflicted on portable computers.

Marina spent some time verifying the sales information by looking at consumer reports and trends in the user community and users' overall purchasing patterns. She suspected that the slowdown would be permanent. Prices had decreased significantly for products using these components, so users were not as concerned about breakage. The products themselves were much lighter and more portable, reducing the requirement for more resilient components. In addition, an overall trend toward leasing rather than buying meant that users were trading in the devices on a regular basis. As a result, component manufacturers were not as concerned about using the higher priced durable components.

> **CII's senior management team recognized that by giving decision-makers at all levels access to the information they needed and enabling them to use that information instantly to validate their decisions, the company could achieve performance breakthroughs right across the business.**

With a 10,000-strong workforce, 20 suppliers, over 50 key clients, and 18 contracted service suppliers spanning the globe, the company works like a moving jigsaw puzzle. The parts need to be in continual proximity, moving in unison, but can never become permanent fixtures since they might have to be juggled again. It is a formula that calls for exceptional foresight and ongoing communication between various players in the system.

The Collaboration Imperative

Given its business model, the integration of employees, suppliers, and customers is an essential business requirement for CII. Driven by information, integration enables people across the value chain to collaborate more effectively—and it enables CII to draw maximum value from every corner of the enterprise.

For example, tracking a product life cycle in the company's client product portfolio calls for linkages not only within CII between sales, production, and marketing, but also between the OEMs and the distributors of the assembled equipment, since each has a different view of the marketplace.

The collaboration between the partners is truly a win–win proposition. All parties have access to the same numbers at the same time, which helps speed up the discussions as well as the decision cycle.

As she explored her sales information, Marina noted that advertising expenditures and sales agent distribution had remained pretty much unchanged over the past six months. She also noted that product returns

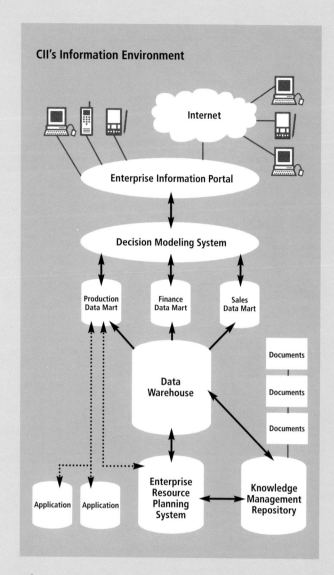

CII's Information Environment

Internet

Enterprise Information Portal

Decision Modeling System

Production Data Mart

Finance Data Mart

Sales Data Mart

Documents

Documents

Documents

Data Warehouse

Application

Application

Enterprise Resource Planning System

Knowledge Management Repository

were up slightly, but that returns to CII from the client had not increased—suggesting that quality was not an issue for CII. But she made a note to talk with her production people in case they had any thoughts about helping the client with its quality control.

With the information she had, it seemed as if customer acceptance of the product was indeed dropping, and companies in the business network associated with this product would probably not be able to increase revenue and profit margins over the next two to three years.

Marina then reviewed another critical information source: the Product Development System (PDS) for Skystone Systems, one of her main customers. Skystone was one of the faster growing manufacturers in the business, and its PDS gave Marina an early view of products the original equipment manufacturer was currently developing. Through the portal, Marina explored Skystone's latest innovation: the P4356. This component was designed for use in the growing market for devices that would integrate telecommunications equipment (for example, cell phones to computers or to personal digital assistants).

Skystone management had a reputation for being very aggressive in tracking new trends in the marketplace and coming up with product ideas to meet the needs. With new products, Skystone expected a quick turnaround and top quality from its contracted assembly partners.

Marina's challenge was to determine whether CII would be able to ramp up production fast enough to capture the business for assembling the P4356. Before bidding on this business, however, she needed assurance that the ToughBoard really was on its way out and wanted a plan that identified how CII would be able to produce the P4356 to meet Skystone's criteria.

As she worked with production data, staff availability, and finance issues, she sifted through a variety of data marts, looking at different intersections of data to get a general idea of how much CII could provide, when, and at what cost.

The Decision Process

Marina's decision process included a series of steps familiar to most businesses: data collection, followed by analysis, and then by a final decision. At CII, the Decision Modeling System now greatly streamlined this process. Marina could gather all the data she needed, conduct the analysis, and send her report electronically to other stakeholders in this decision—without ever leaving her desk. This team might modify some aspects of the decision based on broader strategic concerns, but if the decision was backed by solid data and sound analysis, Marina's recommendations were rarely vetoed by senior management.

In the ToughBoard situation, Marina owned the final decision. However, she also had to be sure that senior managers from all departments involved approved of her plans and that nothing important had been overlooked. It was critical that she share the information upon which she based her decision with other managers in order to avoid spending valuable time talking at cross-purposes or giving lengthy updates and explanations later in the process.

Her decision network also included Skystone Systems, the distributors, and CII's contracted

Creating the Right Information Environment

Managing a business effectively in an environment of constant flux calls for all players to have a solid handle on output requirements and performance metrics at all critical points in the supply chain. But accessing and exploring information from across the value chain hasn't always been easy at CII.

In the past, the right information never seemed to be immediately at hand when people needed it. When a major client had problems with quality, it seemed to take forever to find out what went wrong, where, and who was accountable for making it right. Similarly, if packaging and distribution couldn't meet deadlines, or if the product did not make it to the client in one piece, a lot of running around was required to find out who did what and when.

To tackle the issue, CII had experimented with all of the basic solutions available over the past few years. ERP systems provided a solid foundation but couldn't deal with some of the peculiarities of the business. So custom software for certain areas of the business was often written to beef up the off-the-shelf solution.

CII had also worked with knowledge management. The idea of capturing, cataloging, summarizing, and presenting critical information to people in the organization actually helped focus attention on what people needed to know in order to resolve key issues, so CII had "mapped" relevant corporate knowledge. Still, the overall feeling was that information contained in the knowledge management system was not only pretty static but, more critically, simply not entirely the kind of information needed to accelerate sound decision-making. It was background data but didn't reveal the critical aspects of product success or failure. People found the knowledge management solution too complex, and they wanted relevant, actionable information on what happened this morning to their inventory control in Brazil, not what happened a week ago in a trade journal or at a conference.

CII came to realize that to drive higher performance, it needed decision-makers to view information and make decisions within a common context— a common "truth" or vision. This would help CII employees better understand how their decisions impacted the overall performance of the company.

As CII tackled the issue, there had been numerous discussions about data, information, and knowledge. Eventually, everyone had realized that one person's data is another person's information and might be someone else's knowledge, and that what was important was to have a common context for information, a common understanding of what it meant and how it was to be interpreted at CII. These insights had led to the development of CII's Decision Modeling System. The idea was to put in place a standard process for specific decision-making that would be supported by an information environment that provided access to the data marts, external databanks, the knowledge management system (documents, videos, graphics, and so on) through an Enterprise Information Portal. Everyone understood that the "human process" that mapped people's

staffing supplier, SK Services. These companies all had a stake in CII's decision. Skystone would need to know if CII could deliver, the distributors would have information on how the new products might be received in the marketplace, and the staffing supplier would need to be able to deliver resources to ramp up for production of the new product.

Marina handed the assignment of analyzing the data to Ted Johnstone, a bright young analyst in CII's strategic planning unit. Using the DMS's capabilities for analyzing data then querying specific databases for additional information, Ted collected a wealth of information on the ToughBoard's sales performance, sales agent distribution, and advertising

> **With the DMS, CII decision-makers could collaborate around their decisions rather than around their data, knowing that a decision and its supporting analysis are based on information that is consistent across all departments and shared across the value chain. They could begin to immediately exploit the value of the decision.**

expenditures to validate Marina's initial findings. He also looked in more detail at consumer and industry-specific information sources to review customer buying patterns. The DMS made it easy for Ted to sift through CII's vast data repositories and quickly pinpoint the information "sweet spots" associated with the opportunity at hand, based on the factors and performance indicators that would drive Marina's decision.

The production data marts showed that CII would not have enough slack capacity to take on the new product as well as continue with the others. So Ted searched for other assembly companies that might be interested in subcontracting and provided a ranked list based on quality, turnaround, and price. Finally, he looked through Skystone's Product Development System to check on product specifications for its new offering.

Ted's results confirmed Marina's suspicions. The customer data clearly showed that buyer behavior had changed (owning to leasing), that technology had had an impact (lighter, more portable devices), and that the proliferation of handheld devices (such as palm-tops) was reducing the need for road warriors to lug heavy equipment. Thus, portability was taking precedence over durability.

practices to the technology was absolutely essential to the system actually helping accelerate and improve decision-making.

This idea of a "human process" had developed as business users had worked alongside IT professionals in developing a variety of technology solutions in CII. Like many other organizations in the industry, CII had invested huge sums of money on various systems only to see them fail—not because the technology was not doing what it was supposed to do, but because the human process had not been clearly thought out prior to installation. So CII managers worked hard at understanding the implications of the DMS in terms of their own behaviors.

The Decision

Based on the research information Ted had provided, Marina decided that the company should prepare a formal bid to assemble the P4356. The ToughBoard would also continue to be produced for at least the next fiscal year.

Using the DMS, Marina registered her rationale for the decision: CII's growth projections, along with the impact of the new business on the company's working capital, financial capabilities, and human resources competencies.

DAY 2: SHARING THE RECOMMENDATION AND ITS RATIONALE

Marina knew that her rationale would not be immediately agreeable to every senior executive in the company. The CIO and the COO would have some issues with the way Marina had framed the issue. The CFO would be thinking about the company's cash conversion cycle and the investment required. Finally, the vice president of human resources would want to know about staffing and training requirements in order to develop a plan with SK Services, CII's human resources management contractor.

Developing the Decision Modeling System

The network of partners and stakeholders that formed CII's delivery system had previously been unable to achieve a common understanding of a problem or opportunity within an acceptable time frame. Everyone attributed this to a number of different sources, but people were almost unanimous in their belief that the issue was critical to their ability to function effectively as decision-makers.

Some pointed to information technology as the core problem. They felt that CII's knowledge management system should provide access to all of the information everyone needed, all of the time. But while it is true that knowledge management systems provide information access, they don't necessarily provide a means by which to understand this information or to use it to drive decision-making. In addition, people knew that IT's role is not to tell the company what is important about the business or to determine its strategy. That came from management. IT's role was to reflect the company's strategy in its systems.

Working with a team of external consultants, CII managers and information technology professionals developed the "human process"—the decision culture, in other words—that would best support the collaborative mode of operation required by the business model and complement the improved capability of the company's information technology system. By doing so, CII not only gave its decision-makers an information

technology infrastructure to support decision-making and collaboration (the DMS), but helped to build a decision culture where decision-making would be faster and more efficient.

The Decision Modeling System was more widely adopted by the business community when core guidelines were developed after the first six months of use. These guidelines described how the DMS was to be used and how it would support the day-to-day needs of decision-makers.

Core Guidelines for the DMS:

1. *Every decision is informed by data and context. More than simply business rules and models (which include standard operating procedures, overall company vision, business processes, or general "hurdle rates" for things like capital investments), context at CII also includes past decisions, past relationships between variables in the business, and the changing nature of these relationships. This is to ensure that employees understand the context of their roles within the company's overall strategy and objectives, and that the impact and appropriateness of their decisions are not diluted.*

2. *Decisions must be made before the "point of irrelevance"; that is, before market forces take the decision away. They must be made at the point of maximum impact: typically, the "lowest" possible level in the organization where decision-makers have the knowledge, experience, and understanding to make,*

implement, and monitor a particular decision. With this practice, CII eliminates the upward delegation of decision-making, which can lead to huge bottlenecks in the decision process.

3. Informed decisions are those supported by the quality—rather than the quantity—of the data provided. When people feel they understand the facts and have the validation they need to act, they can make the most effective decision. One of the challenges CII decision-makers face is the sheer volume of information that currently resides in the company's various data repositories. Given the fast-moving nature of the business, CII employees need to be able to efficiently extract high-value, low-volume information and then analyze it quickly and easily. If a specific analysis seems too complicated, then the variables are probably not sufficiently clarified or, alternatively, the tools used to conduct that analysis might lack the appropriate functionality.

4. Impactful decisions require a balanced view of every essential business driver—not just those that focus primarily on financial metrics. They require explicit measurement of less easily quantifiable factors such as customer satisfaction, product innovations, and other less visible, yet no less important, business drivers. Measurable targets and formalized processes must be established in order to track all critical performance indicators.

5. Decisions—at all levels—should not happen in a vacuum. By physically connecting its employees, suppliers, and partners to each other and to the data they need, not only to inform their decisions but also to corroborate them, CII ensures that each decision supports every other decision that is made across its value chain based on consistent rules and a common frame of reference.

6. Outcomes must be monitored. CII management agrees to accept a certain percentage of negative outcomes, knowing that over the long run analyzing these outcomes will help the business make higher quality decisions in a more timely fashion. This, in turn, will help the business prosper. Monitoring decision outcomes includes ensuring that feedback is provided at various levels in the organization, with a continual updating of business rules based on these results. In order to achieve this goal, the people involved have to be open to feedback, willing to model business rules based on success and failure, and capable of establishing cause-and-effect relationships between decisions and outcomes.

Fortunately, divergent perspectives were now viewed as an asset to the decision-making process. One of the hallmarks of the DMS was that all players with input into the decision had to clearly and honestly outline their parameters. They had all learned from experience that hidden agendas in the decision-making process almost always led to uncoordinated decision-making.

Marina packaged her final reports and distributed them via the information portal to each VP or manager responsible for substantiating the decision in light of their own department. It would be these individuals who would make recommendations to their bosses—the CIO, COO, CFO, and VP of HR—about whether or not to support Marina's decision and why. Marina also emphasized in her reports CII's growth targets and the need to react quickly in order to ensure that the transition was as seamless as possible.

The Players

Mike Dawes, VP, Finance

The VP of Finance, Mike Dawes, who reported to CII's CFO, knew that his boss's overall concern would be the dropping revenue and that he would want to maintain growth in what was an extremely competitive marketplace. CII had never competed specifically on price; instead, it sought to deliver high-quality components as quickly as the client needed them with virtually no product defects.

Mike also knew that the CFO held a strong orientation to cash flow management and wanted to avoid financing growth with borrowing, if at all possible. His rationale was that CII had to replace the older products but not with new products that called for extensive capital investment.

> **By interlinking its decision-makers to a network of shared information and a common performance framework, CII was able to accelerate decision validation and execution.**

Understanding this, Mike reviewed the reports Marina had sent. Specifically, he analyzed the estimated "contribution to margin" figures of the new product and the estimated cash flow impact. He compared this option with others, such as cost cutting in production of the ToughBoard to offset the anticipated decrease in costs expected from the client.

Mike focused his attention on the following factors:

- Capital investment required
- Potential cash flow
- Comparison of the options: building a new product; extending the life cycle of the existing product; finding ways to reduce production costs for the ToughBoard
- Profit margin of the new product versus the old
- Potential cannibalization of revenues from other products

Jennifer Hodgson, VP, Operations

As VP of Operations, Jennifer Hodgson cared most about transition. CII had to phase out the ToughBoard and gear up for the new product, and her department would need to ensure that production staff had time to be trained in the new product features, that the systems and processes could meet quality and delivery time specs, and that the ratio of capital to labor was reasonable. Her main issue was whether the investment in capital or in staff training could be leveraged to other products or other processes in the future. She also had issues with space: specifically, whether or not a new plant would be required, or whether CII would use overtime or hire new people from SK Services. Overtime would not require additional space, but could reduce productivity if it went on too long. Hiring new people would require additional space, but would likely maintain productivity—apart from the learning curve that new hires always encounter. Still, SK Services could help with the training, and that would reduce the performance decrements often noted early in the learning curve.

Jennifer's main concerns were as follows:

- Relative combination of capital versus labor
- Retooling and retraining required
- Capacity: should this be outsourced?

Kathryn McLeary, Director, Information Technology

As a direct report to the CIO, Kathryn was mainly concerned about ensuring that the

Nurturing an Open, Flexible Decision Culture

CII's managers realized that it was critical to the company's overall success that they nurture and develop an open, dynamic, and flexible decision culture in tandem with implementing the technical aspects of the DMS. One of the central benefits of this approach was that, over time, it greatly improved trust among decision-makers.

Like many organizations, CII had been a company in which managers needed to be careful about "managing impressions." In the past, they had been very careful never to openly admit mistakes for fear of jeopardizing their careers. This made it very difficult to accurately measure and effectively manage business performance. People were continually working with inaccurate or inconsistent data that did not match up with the numbers held by others. This scenario not only often led to highly uncoordinated, ineffective decision-making, but also created a culture of mistrust around decision-making. As a result, any key decision could be arbitrarily halted or challenged, ultimately paralyzing the smooth operation of the company.

Within this cultural framework, a DMS would never work effectively. Because it captures hard data as well as people's intuitions, because some of the most important lessons learned are derived from failures, and because the people who make these decisions need to be directly involved in updating the business rules to avoid similar errors in the future, the DMS needed to be built on the foundation of personal accountability, trust, and teamwork to succeed.

Streamlining the Decision-Making Process

Now, once a decision was made, outcomes were carefully tracked because these would inform subsequent decisions. In some cases, for example, the business rules that formed the context for a decision might have to be changed, but CII management would know this only if it knew the result of a particular decision.

This streamlined approach to decision-making had taken some time and effort to develop. In years past, CII had suffered from tight bottlenecks and committee-style decision-making practices. For example, the decision to outsource HR staffing and training services had been fraught with people arguing from different information sources. The VP of HR at the time had figures for training costs that did not match the figures the CFO had; nor did the rolled-up figures from CII's regions reconcile with those of the CFO or of the VP.

Therefore, the VP had argued that expenses were as low as they could be, while the CFO showed his figures demonstrating that costs were increasing rapidly. Regional managers were at a loss to figure out how much they were spending, so they had no idea if the contractor approach would improve service and contain costs. It had taken almost eight months to get the right information, to clarify the business case, and to determine which option would provide more value. Moreover, the decision context was clouded by the suspicion that the VP of HR was trying to protect an empire as opposed to looking at what was best for the

characteristics of the new product could be modeled effectively into the DMS. There was no point in producing something if its performance could not be tracked or if there was not enough time to ensure that its profitability could be effectively analyzed beforehand.

Before making any recommendation to her boss, Kathryn had to review Skystone Systems' Product Development System (PDS) to see what the specifics of the new product might be. She wanted to be able to model it effectively in CII's DMS. It didn't look as though she would have to change much in terms of database structures, but she noted that costs of producing the P4356 might be higher than other products because of additional components. She also wanted to be sure that the transaction system would capture the additional cost categories for the P4356 components.

Jack Donata, VP, Human Resources

Based on an overview of Marina's report provided by one of his senior HR managers, Jack Donata knew that CII's staffing supplier, SK Services, would have a major problem if more staff were needed. It would have to recruit, which would increase training and orientation costs. Attracting new staff is a critical issue for most organizations. Jack reviewed SK Services' current load and capacity and pored over the various scenarios for different levels of staffing requirements. The key concerns he was presented with were:

- Number of new staff needed
- Adjustments required to the arrangement with SK Services to provide this staff
- Training needed for contracted staff as well as for CII staff involved in production
- Impact of overtime, if required, on its contract arrangements as well as employee morale
- Migration of staff from the ToughBoard to the P4356 as the time came to phase out the ToughBoard

Validating Marina's Recommendation

Upon discussing with each of their senior officers the findings and recommendations related to the impact of Marina's activities on their individual departments, each VP or manager responded to Marina's report by providing an outline

> **The DMS enabled CII to minimize the upward delegation of decisions by empowering those who are closer to the point of impact and, in reality, should own the decision. Decision-makers could now access the appropriate information in a way that would not only inform their decision but also help them understand the repercussions of their decision on their department as well on the rest of the company.**

of his or her rationale and immediate and long-term concerns. They not only provided additional data but added case histories of similar decisions in the past and the outcomes (these had been monitored and captured in the DMS). Marina reviewed the information and

business. Thus, people around the table were working with different data, different business rules, and an underlying sense of mistrust and hidden agendas. The management team knew that this type of decision-making simply had to change if the company was to keep pace with its competitors. Most of the businesses in the industry had already contracted out a number of internal services and had realized benefits in terms of flexibility and adaptability. While CII senior managers were still arguing among themselves, its main competitor, Boring Lang Inc., had managed to reduce operating costs and, by reducing its fees, capture a number of key clients that CII had also been courting.

So the senior management team, under the leadership of the CEO, had taken a much more serious approach to understanding and developing its decision-making processes. In order to develop a common understanding of purpose and personal accountability, CII management, working with consultants from a leading technology company, clearly identified the owners of various types of decision points. For example, senior product managers now "owned" decisions related to product strategy. They consulted with other key stakeholders but it was ultimately the strength of their business case that would form the basis of any decision made by senior management to green-light or put off a given project.

Aligning the Decision-Making Process and the DMS

This concept of personal accountability and responsibility was also built into the technical support side of the DMS. During the development of the portal, the roles of various positions in the company were clearly identified, decision-making responsibilities were defined for those business roles, and everyone in the decision network was made fully aware of these roles and the related decision-making responsibilities. The portal delivered preset information to every decision-maker each morning, based on each person's business role and decision-making responsibilities.

Developing the system in this way helped to ensure that decisions are always made at the point of greatest impact; the decision owner gathers information that is critical to his or her decision; colleagues are involved in feeding the process, but everyone recognizes who has to make the final call. Once a decision is made, "ownership" implies monitoring and follow-up. Hence the DMS was constantly enriched by modeling and encapsulating not only the operational thresholds based on key performance indicators but also the outcomes of decisions into the system so that it could effectively inform future decisions. In this way, CII could ensure that all key business drivers operated at peak performance.

A New Decision Culture

This culture called for senior managers to avoid micro-managing and for decision-makers at all

forwarded the package to Ted for further analysis and preparation of the final report.

Independent but Shared Analysis of the Problem

By combining information received from each department's knowledge of CII's Operations, Ted was able to generate a summary report on behalf of the team.

The facts were as follows:

- ToughBoard sales had increased by 15% over the past year, but the Profit and Loss Chart(PLC) showed a declining acceleration suggesting that it would peak in about a year or so. It would still contribute to revenues for about four to five years, but two years from now it would no longer be a strong performer.

- The new product would not necessarily require new capital investment but would require an increase of 15% in labor to meet the quality and production timing requirements.

- It might be possible to lower this increase with strategic capital outlay for advanced CAM equipment, but the new machinery could not be applied to other products.

- The gross margin for the new product was approximately 12% more than the current ToughBoard product. Ramping up the new product as the older product was declining, CII could ensure that the drop-off of ToughBoard pretty much matched the growth phase of the new product, thus maintaining revenue growth and profitability.

Although the decision was arrived at in a shared manner, all team members knew that Marina was ultimately responsible for making the final recommendation to the CEO about whether to proceed.

Once this decision was made, each department would make further decisions around implementation that would entail lower level operational decisions. Each decision-maker focused on his or her own decision responsibility and allowed subsequent players in the business unit to follow through as needed. Because they had all received the initial information, they knew of the pending decision, and many were already preparing contingency plans to put the decision into action.

After reviewing the data, it became clear to all that the ToughBoard would continue to sell for some time, but the year-over-year deceleration in sales volume increase definitely showed a product that would mature in about a year, with a concomitant drop in profit margin.

levels to realize that they were accountable for a decision and had the authority to intelligently contribute to their component of the company's overall performance goals.

The transition was not easy; some managers never quite adjusted to the new system. These were managers who would, in the past, allocate budgets to their subordinates but require these employees to justify any major decision with voluminous business cases. In the new business environment, justification was still necessary but, by the time the decision was made, all managers with a stake in the decision already knew why because they were fully involved through the DMS. More importantly, the delay introduced by the former process of "business case, presentation, deliberation, final decision" was avoided. The DMS was a visible manifestation of the culture of empowerment developed in CII.

The conclusions were unarguable:

- The ToughBoard could not help maintain revenue growth in the long run.
- Market information for the new product demonstrated a high take-up rate.
- The phasing out of ToughBoard would not happen immediately; thus the phase-in of the new product could happen gradually. At some point, the contribution curves would cross, allowing for complete phase-out.
- Maintaining growth was critical to the long-term future of CII.

DAY 3: MAKING DECISIONS

Marina had scheduled a meeting to discuss the final decision. The team met at 8:30 on the morning of Day 3 of the decision process. Marina asked if anyone had any outstanding issues and made it clear that, in her opinion, they should proceed with a bid for the new product. She thought that contracting out might be the best way to go, but knew that Jennifer Hodgson's operations staff would determine how best to tackle the production issue. After a brief discussion, the meeting adjourned and each of the department representatives focused attention on the decisions required in their units to implement the new product assembly.

The most critical aspect now was to decide on contracting out or relying on in-house production. The VP of Operations, Jennifer Hodgson, used the portal to borrow the cost-benefit calculations prepared by Mike Dawes in Finance and worked with the senior manager of HR on staffing issues. The challenge was figuring out how much product to build so that the initial staffing requirements could be kept within parameters that SK Services could handle.

Of course, Skystone was also involved. It had certain timing issues that had to be respected. But since it was in the early stages of product development, production numbers could initially be kept low, giving CII some valuable breathing room.

Operations, Finance, and HR each provided Ted Johnstone, Marina's analyst, with a series of requirements in terms of investment, staffing, time to market, and product launch. Ted worked with operations people in SK Services and Skystone to determine numbers on production volume and timing. Jennifer tapped one of her senior operations managers to work with Ted to ensure that practical realities of CII's operating environment were taken into account. From IT, Kathyrn McLeary sent along a team member to capture information that would need to be modeled into the DMS.

> **CII understood early on that the DMS must do more than connect people to the business by uniting previously disparate islands of data and ensuring a coordinated, integrated view of the business. It also had to be able to drive data out to employees while providing the means to conduct multidimensional analyses of key performance indicators— all in real time.**

As each decision was made, monitoring and feedback mechanisms were added and adjusted. For example, since the P4356 required specific types of wiring that were more costly than wiring used in CII's current products, information on new suppliers was entered into the DMS. Similarly, the expected gross margin ranges had to be modified for this specific product and for the product portfolio as a whole since the average expected gross margin would be affected.

The decision process replicated itself along the various decision roles in the organization. Marina, with guidance from her boss, the senior vice president of Marketing, owned the strategic decision, which she made with support and feedback from each department. They in turn inherited a series of more tactical decisions, which they made based on data collection, team input, and feedback from their colleagues.

At each stage, measurable indicators were developed and modeled into the DMS to ensure that tracking of outcomes would be possible. Information collected would be used to modify business rules. For example, current production methods were based mostly on internal assembly. The outsourcing tactic might have a different impact on gross margin that could then be modeled in the DMS so that future decisions could benefit from current activities.

Marina was kept abreast of the series of decisions that followed hers. Typically, she would intervene only if she thought something would impact CII's ability to get this product out on time with the required quality. Her involvement would not be to make a decision, but rather to influence the rationale by which the decision-owner at that point of impact came to a decision.

DAY 4: IMPLEMENTING DECISIONS

In IT, Kathryn McLeary's staff updated CII's intranet to reflect the new product offering. They also updated the various databases to reflect the new product and ensured that key performance indicators for each stage in the implementation process were modeled in the managers' and officers' personalized portals. Some of these indicators were delivered from SK Services (staffing costs, training and development, competency development in new production capabilities).

Key factors that needed to be tracked as the product ramped up included:

- Labor costs
- Adoption rate
- Production downtime and overtime
- Revenue

Based on the recommendations of her senior manager, Jennifer Hodgson agreed that outsourcing of assembly was the best way to go. Her production manager began negotiation with one of the assembly business partners to develop options on how best to structure this relationship.

The series of decisions that were made in each of the functional areas was communicated to the management team through the DMS. For example, the outcomes of negotiations with the assembly partners would have an impact on production costs. Mike Dawes needed to know this sooner rather than later in order to adjust his financial projections. Similarly, HR needed to know so that it might make adjustments in its negotiations with the staffing contractor in order to keep production costs within the agreed-upon parameters.

Overall, Marina needed to stay up-to-date with the aggregate impact of the various decisions in the functional areas. In her role as decision-owner, she also had the responsibility for making adjustments on the fly when she recognized the impact these decisions could have on CII's ability to meet the client's expectations. The DMS allowed for near real-time tracking of the outcomes in each of the functional areas (the time lag was due to many of the managers not wanting to record decisions until they were sure that these were in final form; sometimes, Marina would receive e-mailed updates informing her of a pending change).

DAY 5: CLOSING THE LOOP ON THE DECISION

The ultimate impact that CII sought with this decision was to keep its revenue growth on track. To assess the effectiveness of the decision in meeting this goal, CII had to be able to understand the outcome of the decision and attribute a cause-and-effect relationship between this outcome and the decision's overall impact.

As decisions continued to be made, each unit in the organization was made aware of the anticipated impact but also had a clear understanding of the key performance indicators within it. For example, production tracked the costs of producing the new product, HR tracked staffing and training costs as well as competency development, and finance tracked revenues and contribution directly attributable to the new product.

Once the deal was made with the subcontractor for assembly, continued monitoring of impact and outcomes over time would allow CII to refresh and update some of its business rules. It would learn, for example, that while subcontracting eliminated the costs of staff training and recruitment, it also called for enhanced monitoring and contract management. CII had subcontracted before, but never for a new product, so this aspect would be modeled into the system to inform future decisions, much as past decisions on product abandonment were used to inform this decision.

At the same time, information on the ToughBoard was still being gathered, so the comparison allowed CII to continue to determine whether the new product was doing what it was supposed to do in terms of revenue growth.

Determining whether the decision to move ahead with the P4356 was a success or a failure would not be possible until the P4356 had had an opportunity to demonstrate its impact on revenue, so the team postponed that discussion until ramp up and product launch. The DMS, in this case, served as a reminder to all that this critical loop had to be closed at a specific time in the future.

If revenue growth were to slow down, determining whether the decision was successful would become more complex. In this case, the power of the DMS would really be demonstrated because it would allow CII managers to look at the various factors that drive sales and margins of the new product. Using this capability, CII could find out if operating costs were too high, if the market had shifted before the product hit, or if a substitute product had reduced its sales potential by beating its product to market.

THE BOTTOM LINE

By distributing *de facto* decision-making power to the person closest to each decision's outcome and operating with a shared understanding of the goals and outcomes of each decision, CII has been able to significantly accelerate the decision process, and therefore the company's overall business performance.

But, as valuable and essential as this is to CII, the senior management team feels that the real competitive advantage is the system's ability to trigger a decision in the first place. That is, because each member of the network continually receives a flow of key performance indicators, and each can drill down and across various data sets to find reasons for variances, managers in CII are now beginning to anticipate problems well before the situation becomes a crisis and seize opportunities before the competition does.

In the case of the ToughBoard decision, the volume deceleration flag had alerted Marina to a product's imminent maturity, allowing her to proactively search for new products that would fit with the company's current portfolio as well as with its revenue targets. Speedy discovery and action also meant that CII could capitalize on the P4356 opportunity before it disappeared. Skytone Systems could have gone to a competitor had CII been unable to come to a decision quickly.

The decision process had been efficient. Once the team agreed on the main decision, operational decisions flowed quickly within the framework and business rules created by the strategic decision. All in all, the senior management team at CII felt that its previous decision-making process had been quite archaic compared with the approach built into the DMS. The system proved itself every day, at every level of management in CII.

DAY 1	DAY 2	DAY 3	DAY 4	DAY 5
Discovery and analysis	*Sharing the recommendation and its rationale*	*Making decisions*	*Implementing decisions*	*Closing the loop on the decision*

ACKNOWLEDGMENTS

Developing this book was a fascinating project. It required the discipline to analyze and synthesize what I have learned from my many years of working with large and small organizations as they strive to better understand what's driving their business and how they can better manage its performance. And it called for further validation of some of the thinking through additional research.

I would like to acknowledge the many outstanding individuals and companies who have been willing to openly share with us the challenges they face in continually optimizing the performance of their business and their strategies to win, most particularly the small subset whose experiences are mentioned in this book to illustrate our principles in action: Gary Loveman, Chief Operating Officer at Harrah's Entertainment, Inc.; Gordon Khan, Senior Vice President and Chief Financial Officer, Hunter Douglas North America; Mark Hurd, President, NCR Corporation and Chief Operating Officer, Teradata Division; and Bill Braddy, Vice President of Engineering and Knowledge Services at Schneider Logistics. Since their insights touch on management challenges that are often carefully guarded within an organization, I am grateful that they would share their experiences with me and with the readers of this book.

I am also deeply indebted to brilliant management thinkers such as Peter Drucker, Gary Hamel, Michael Hammer, Geoffrey Moore, and Tom Peters, who have been the most influential in setting the foundation for business management as we know it today. To Robin McNeill, Richard Connelly, and Roland Mosimann, authors of The Multi-dimensional Manager, *the revolutionary book that highlighted the critical importance of delivering business information that maps to the way managers think about the business. And to Don Tapscott and Digital 4Sight, whose work on the digital economy clearly outlines the new challenges organizations face as they compete in the new internetworked era.*

Special thanks go to Shannon Ross, who contributed enormously to the process of developing "Smooth Sailing on Rough Seas." Shannon is a gifted business writer who helped to solidify the book's main concepts and apply these to our eight principles, communicating these ideas simply and effectively through clear, well-structured narrative. Her work has resulted in what we believe to be a compelling read for business managers. Thanks also to Greg Richards, Ph.D., whose unique blend of business and technology knowledge helped us build a case study that illustrates the overall business impact of all of the principles, and to the other members of our editorial team—Terence Atkinson, Meg Dussault, Lyse Teasdale, and Karen Williams—for their insistence on "getting it right."

And finally, I would like to thank Marshall Warwaruk, Larry DeBoever, Alan Rottenberg, Rob Ashe, Terry Hall, and Ron Zambonini, who all fostered my sense of "what's going on" and, most importantly, told me to tell others about it.